MOVIE ★ ICONS

EASTWOOD

EDITOR
PAUL DUNCAN

TEXT
DOUGLAS KEESEY

PHOTOS
THE KOBAL COLLECTION

TASCHEN

HONG KONG KÖLN LONDON LOS ANGELES MADRID PARIS TOKYO

CONTENTS

1

CLINT EASTWOOD: MYTHIC MACHISMO

BY DOUGLAS KEESEY

CLINT EASTWOOD: MACHO UND MYTHOS

CLINT EASTWOOD : LE MYTHE DU MACHO

CLINT EASTWOOD: MYTHIC MACHISMO

by Douglas Keesey

Tall, laconic, and lethal, the ruthless gunslinger known as The Man with No Name was Clint Eastwood's first great screen persona. Appearing in three spaghetti Westerns – *A Fistful of Dollars* (1964), *For a Few Dollars More* (1965), and *The Good, the Bad and the Ugly* (1966) – this brutal antihero was an iconic image carefully constructed by Eastwood and director Sergio Leone. First, Eastwood's 6-foot, 4-inch height made him a towering presence; the actor notes that he has been compared to a small redwood tree. Then the squinty eyes, grizzled face, and ragged poncho gave him a mean look, not to mention the thin Mexican cigars that Eastwood hated to smoke and that put him in a sour frame of mind. Leone advised the actor, "Don't just do something, stand there," and Eastwood's tense stillness conveyed the sense of a gathering rage about to explode from his Colt .45. Eastwood cut his own dialogue to create an omnipresent sense of menace – "He let the air speak louder than the words," said Quincy Jones – and when he did speak, Eastwood hissed his threats through clenched teeth. The film's producers were initially skeptical. As Eastwood reports, they said, "Christ, this guy isn't doing anything. He isn't saying anything. He doesn't even have a name! And that cigar is just sitting there burning." But audiences all over the world responded to the powerful mystique conveyed by Eastwood's minimalist approach to character creation.

Although he would go by different names, Eastwood essentially continued this role of the vicious and invincible gunfighter in such Hollywood films as *High Plains Drifter* (1973), where he

PAGES 2/3
PORTRAIT FOR 'THE ENFORCER' (1976)

PAGE 4
PORTRAIT

PAGE 6
STILL FROM 'FOR A FEW DOLLARS MORE' (1965)

STILL FROM 'DIRTY HARRY' (1971)
The cop as urban cowboy, solving crimes by killing the culprits. / Der Polizist als Stadtcowboy, der Verbrechen aufklärt, indem er die Schuldigen abknallt. / Un cow-boy urbain qui mène l'enquête en abattant les coupables.

"I don't like killing. It's one thing to fantasize about it in a movie, but I never saw the sport in removing a life from the planet."
Clint Eastwood

wreaked vengeance on cowardly townsfolk by having the town painted red as Hell and then, rather than saving it from the villains, watched while it was destroyed, and *Pale Rider* (1985), where he played a Preacher who dispensed unholy justice as if he were one of the Four Horsemen of the Apocalypse. But Eastwood also showed a willingness to humanize his heroic image. In *The Outlaw Josey Wales* (1976), Eastwood's lone gunman became more sociable by joining a ragtag community of women, bonding with a Cherokee elder, and adopting a stray dog, while in *Bronco Billy* (1980) Eastwood poked fun at his mythic machismo by playing an ex-shoe salesman who billed himself as "the fastest gun in the West" in a carnival sideshow. By the time of *Unforgiven* (1992), Eastwood really set out to demythologize the Western 'hero' and his 'righteous' violence: "I've done as much as the next person as far as creating mayhem in Westerns," Eastwood said, "but what I like about *Unforgiven* is that every killing in it has a repercussion. It really tears people up when they are violent." Eastwood starred as reformed gunfighter William Munny, who is haunted by visions of the worm-eaten bodies of men he has shot. At the end of the film, Munny is driven by revenge to kill again. His victim's last words are "I'll see you in Hell."

Eastwood's other most famous persona was a kind of urban cowboy – the rogue cop 'Dirty' Harry Callahan, known for his loose-cannon impatience with search warrants, Miranda rights, and other legal technicalities that too often let the guilty go free. Iconic moments include the ones where Harry would point his .44 Magnum at suspects and dare them to make a move that would "force" him to shoot: "I know what you're thinking: 'Did he fire six shots or only five?… Do I feel lucky?' Well, do you, punk?"; and "Go ahead, make my day." Harry seemed to blow away crooks with such righteous relish that critics like Pauline Kael accused *Dirty Harry* (1971) of being a fascist film promoting vigilante violence, and others attacked the movie for casting racial minorities as criminals, and women as weak victims in need of rescue by a man. To counter these charges, Eastwood recalibrated Harry's image for the sequels. In *The Dead Pool* (1988), Harry was teamed up with an Asian partner, and in *The Enforcer* (1976), Harry gained respect for a strong female partner who good-naturedly mocked his machismo by calling him "cold, bold Callahan with his great big .44." In *Sudden Impact* (1983), Harry not only let a female serial killer go, he aided her in taking revenge on the men who had gang-raped her. And in *Magnum Force* (1973), Harry stood up against a group of renegade cops who, as he had done in the past, used their .44 Magnums to enforce vigilante justice. Thus Eastwood's image has changed with the times, in accordance with what his father once told him: "You either progress or you decay."

PAGES 8/9
STILL FROM 'THE GOOD, THE BAD AND THE UGLY' (1968)

STILL FROM 'HANG 'EM HIGH' (1968)
Blasting away: Eastwood as righteous lawman or violent outlaw? / Feuer frei: Eastwood als rechtschaffener Gesetzeshüter oder brutaler Gesetzloser? / Fusillade : Eastwood en justicier ou en hors-la-loi ?

CLINT EASTWOOD: MACHO UND MYTHOS

von Douglas Keesey

Der „Namenlose", ein großer, lakonischer, skrupelloser, unbarmherziger Revolverheld, war Clint Eastwoods erste große Leinwandfigur. Der brutale Antiheld trat in drei Spaghettiwestern auf – *Für eine Handvoll Dollar* (1964), *Für ein paar Dollar mehr* (1965) und *Zwei glorreiche Halunken* (1966) – und war ein von Eastwood und Regisseur Sergio Leone sorgfältig aufgebautes Image. Zum einen war Eastwood durch seine Körpergröße von 1,93 m schon eine stattliche Erscheinung – er behauptet, man habe ihn damals mit einem kleinen Mammutbaum verglichen. Dann waren da die zusammengekniffenen Augen, das stoppelbärtige Gesicht und der zerlumpte Poncho, die ihn besonders böse aussehen ließen, ganz zu schweigen von den mexikanischen Zigarillos, die Eastwood hasste und die ihm die Laune verdarben. Leone wies den Schauspieler ausdrücklich an: „Mach nicht immer irgendwas, steh einfach da", und Eastwoods spannungsgeladene Stille vermittelte ein Gefühl der Wut, die sich langsam aufstaute und sich bald darauf aus seinem 45er Colt entladen würde. Eastwood kürzte seine eigenen Dialoge, um ein allgegenwärtiges Gefühl der Bedrohung zu erzeugen – „bei ihm sprach die Luft lauter als die Worte", sagte Quincy Jones –, und wenn er sprach, zischte er seine Drohungen durch zusammengebissene Zähne. Anfangs waren die Produzenten der Filme skeptisch. Eastwood zufolge sagten sie: „Herrgott, der Kerl tut ja nichts. Er sagt nichts. Er hat nicht mal einen Namen! Und die Zigarre brennt nur runter." Aber das Publikum in aller Welt reagierte wohlwollend auf die mächtige Aura, die Eastwoods minimalistischer Ansatz in der Charakterdarstellung ausstrahlte.

Unter verschiedenen Namen spielte Eastwood weiterhin die Rolle des unmoralischen, unbesiegbaren Revolverhelden in Hollywoodfilmen. So erteilt er in *Ein Fremder ohne Namen* (1973) feigen Bürgern eine Lektion, indem er ihre Stadt rot wie die Hölle anmalt und dann zuschaut, wie sie zerstört wird, statt sie vor den Bösewichtern zu retten. In *Pale Rider – Der namenlose Reiter* (1985) spielt er einen Prediger, der auf recht unheilige Weise Recht spricht, als sei er einer der vier apokalyptischen Reiter. Aber Eastwood war auch willens, sein Heldenimage zu vermenschlichen. In *Der Texaner* (1976) zeigt sich der einzelgängerische Revolverheld

„Ich mag Töten nicht. In einem Film darüber zu phantasieren, das ist eine Sache, aber ich fand es noch nie lustig, ein Leben von diesem Planeten zu entfernen."
Clint Eastwood

PORTRAIT FOR 'THE ENFORCER' (1976)
The Dirty Harry dare: "Go ahead, make my day." / Dirty Harrys Herausforderung: „Na los, mach mich glücklich." / Le célèbre défi de l'inspecteur Harry : « Vas-y, fais-moi plaisir. »

schon geselliger: Er tut sich mit einer bunt zusammengewürfelten Gruppe von Frauen zusammen, freundet sich mit einem Cherokee-Ältesten an und nimmt einen streunenden Hund auf. In *Bronco Billy* (1980) machte sich Eastwood sogar über seinen Macho-Mythos lustig, indem er einen ehemaligen Schuhverkäufer spielt, der sich auf dem Jahrmarkt als „der schnellste Schütze im Westen" anpreist. Als dann die Zeit reif war für *Erbarmungslos* (1992), machte Eastwood es sich endgültig zur Aufgabe, den Mythos des Western-„Helden" und seiner „gerechtfertigten" Gewalt zu zerstören: „Ich bin genauso verantwortlich für die Western-Metzeleien wie viele andere", sagte Eastwood, „aber was mir an *Erbarmungslos* gefällt, ist, dass jede Tötung Auswirkungen hat. Es zerstört die Menschen, wenn sie Gewalt ausüben." Eastwood spielt den bekehrten Revolverhelden William Munny, den die wurmzerfressenen Leichen seiner Opfer in Alpträumen heimsuchen. Am Ende des Films treibt die Rache Munny wieder zum Töten. Die letzten Worte des Mannes, den er erschießt, sind: „Ich seh dich in der Hölle wieder!"

Eastwoods zweite berühmte Leinwandfigur war eine Art Stadtcowboy: der unkonventionelle Polizist „Dirty" Harry Callahan. Er ist bekannt für seinen lockeren Finger am Abzug und seine Ungeduld mit Durchsuchungsbefehlen, den Rechten von Festgenommenen und anderen technischen Feinheiten, durch die die Schuldigen nur allzuoft wieder auf freien Fuß kommen. In inzwischen klassischen Momenten zielt Harry mit seiner 44er Magnum auf Tatverdächtige und fordert sie zu Handlungen heraus, die ihn zum Schießen „zwingen" würden: „Ich weiß, was du denkst: ‚Hat er sechs Schüsse abgegeben oder nur fünf? ... Hab ich heute meinen Glückstag?' Na, was meinst du, Punk?" und „Na los schon, mach mich glücklich!" Harry schien die Gauner mit solch selbstgerechter Wonne abzuknallen, dass Kritiker wie Pauline Kael *Dirty Harry* (1971) als faschistischen Film beschimpften, der brutale Selbstjustiz propagiere. Andere warfen dem Film dagegen vor, er besetze die Rollen von Kriminellen mit rassischen Minderheiten und stelle Frauen als schwache Opfer dar, die von einem Mann gerettet werden müssten. In Reaktion auf diese Vorwürfe passte Eastwood in den Fortsetzungen Harrys Image an. In *Das Todesspiel* (1988) erhält Harry einen asiatischen Partner, und in *Der Unerbittliche* (1976) lernt Harry, eine starke Partnerin zu respektieren, die seinen Machismo wohlwollend bespöttelt, indem sie Harry als „kalten, kühlen Callahan mit seiner großen, dicken 44er" bezeichnet. In *Dirty Harry kommt zurück* (1983) lässt Harry nicht nur eine Serienmörderin laufen, sondern hilft ihr sogar noch, sich an den Männern zu rächen, die sie nacheinander vergewaltigt hatten. Und in *Calahan* (1973) stellt sich Harry einer Bande abtrünniger Polizisten entgegen, die – wie er selbst in der Vergangenheit – ihre 44er Magnums benutzt hatten, um Selbstjustiz zu üben. So hat sich Eastwoods Image mit der Zeit gewandelt, ganz so, wie es ihm sein Vater einst geraten hatte: „Entweder du entwickelst dich weiter, oder du gehst kaputt."

ON THE SET OF 'TWO MULES FOR SISTER SARA' (1970)

Eastwood directed by his mentor Don Siegel, with Shirley MacLaine. / Eastwood mit Shirley MacLaine unter der Regie seines Mentors Don Siegel. / Eastwood dirigé par son mentor, Don Siegel, en compagnie de Shirley MacLaine.

CLINT EASTWOOD : LE MYTHE DU MACHO

Douglas Keesey

Aussi brutal que laconique, l'impitoyable flingueur surnommé l'Homme sans nom est le premier grand personnage de Clint Eastwood à l'écran. Présent dans trois westerns spaghetti – *Pour une poignée de dollars* (1964), *Et pour quelques dollars de plus* (1965) et *Le Bon, la Brute et le Truand* (1966) –, ce redoutable antihéros est un mythe méticuleusement élaboré par l'acteur avec le metteur en scène Sergio Leone. Tout d'abord, sa taille (1 mètre 93) lui confère une présence imposante qui lui vaudra d'être qualifié de « petit séquoia ». Ensuite, ses yeux plissés, son visage buriné et son poncho élimé lui donnent un air mauvais, sans parler des cigarillos mexicains que l'acteur déteste et qui le mettent de méchante humeur. Sur les conseils de Sergio Leone, Eastwood mise tout sur sa simple présence et son immobilité rend palpable la tension qui monte, prête à fuser de son colt 45. Pour souligner cette menace omniprésente, Eastwood tronque ses propres répliques, « laissant l'air faire plus de bruit que les mots », comme dirait Quincy Jones. Et lorsqu'il se décide à parler, il profère des menaces sans desserrer les dents. Au départ, les producteurs se montrent sceptiques. Comme le raconte Eastwood, ils ont du mal à concevoir un héros qui ne fait rien, ne dit rien, n'a même pas de nom et dont le cigare se consume tout seul. Mais le public du monde entier sera sensible au personnage mythique né du jeu minimaliste de Clint Eastwood.

Même s'il porte différents noms, Eastwood continue globalement à incarner le même personnage de tueur invincible dans diverses productions hollywoodiennes. Dans *L'Homme des hautes plaines* (1973), il se venge de la lâcheté des habitants d'une bourgade en la faisant repeindre en rouge et rebaptiser « L'Enfer » et en assistant tranquillement à sa destruction plutôt que de la protéger contre les brigands. Dans *Pale Rider, le cavalier solitaire* (1985), il incarne un pasteur qui dispense une justice bien peu divine tel un cavalier de l'Apocalypse. Mais Eastwood se montre également désireux d'humaniser son image. Dans *Josey Wales hors-la-loi* (1976), son personnage de cow-boy solitaire devient plus sociable ; il rejoint une communauté de pauvres gueuses, se lie à un patriarche cherokee et adopte un chien errant. Dans *Bronco Billy* (1980), Eastwood tourne en dérision son image de macho

STILL FROM 'COOGAN'S BLUFF' (1968)
Bloody but not beaten, Eastwood's physicality triumphs in the end. / Blutverschmiert, aber ungeschlagen triumphiert Eastwood durch seine körperliche Überlegenheit. / Blessé mais pas vaincu, il finira par triompher.

« Je n'aime pas tuer. C'est une chose de fantasmer là-dessus dans un film, mais je ne vois vraiment pas l'intérêt de supprimer une vie de cette planète. »
Clint Eastwood

en interprétant un ancien marchand de chaussures qui se présente comme « le meilleur tireur de l'Ouest » dans une foire ambulante. Lorsqu'il tourne *Impitoyable* (1992), Eastwood est bien décidé à démythifier le « héros » de western et sa violence « vertueuse » : « J'ai fait couler autant de sang qu'un autre dans les westerns, explique-t-il, mais ce qui me plaît dans *Impitoyable*, c'est que chaque meurtre a des répercussions. La violence fait réellement souffrir les gens. » Eastwood y incarne William Munny, un tueur repentant hanté par la vision des corps de ses victimes dévorés par les vers. À la fin du film, la soif de vengeance le conduit à commettre un nouveau meurtre et les derniers mots de sa victime sont « On se reverra en enfer ».

L'autre personnage le plus célèbre de Clint Eastwood est l'inspecteur Harry Callahan, sorte de cow-boy urbain réputé pour ses méthodes de franc-tireur et son mépris pour les mandats de perquisition, les droits de l'accusé et autres formalités juridiques permettant au coupable de s'en tirer. Les scènes où l'inspecteur Harry pointe son 44 Magnum sur un suspect et le défie de faire le moindre geste qui le « forcerait » à tirer sont entrées dans la légende avec leurs célèbres répliques « Vas-y, fais-moi plaisir » ou « Je sais ce que tu te demandes : "Est-ce qu'il a tiré six coups ou seulement cinq ?... Je tente ma chance ou pas ?" Alors, tu la tentes, ta chance ? » Il semble éliminer la racaille avec une telle délectation que des critiques comme Pauline Kael accusent *L'Inspecteur Harry* (1971) d'être un film fasciste faisant l'apologie de la violence et de l'autodéfense, tandis que d'autres lui reprochent de ne représenter les minorités raciales que comme des criminels et les femmes comme des victimes impuissantes sauvées par un homme. Pour contrer ces accusations, Eastwood recadre l'image de l'inspecteur Harry dans les films suivants. Dans *La Dernière Cible* (1988), Harry fait équipe avec un collègue d'origine asiatique, tandis que dans *L'inspecteur ne renonce jamais* (1976), sa partenaire gagne son respect et se moque de ses airs de macho froid et intrépide brandissant son gros Magnum. Dans *Le Retour de l'inspecteur Harry* (1983), ce dernier laisse non seulement filer une tueuse en série, mais il l'aide même à se venger des hommes qui l'on violée. Et dans *Magnum Force* (1973), il se dresse contre une bande de flics rebelles qui, comme il l'a fait par le passé, rendent une justice expéditive à l'aide de leurs armes. Fidèle au précepte de son père (« Qui ne progresse pas recule »), Clint Eastwood a su évoluer avec le temps.

STILL FROM 'ANY WHICH WAY YOU CAN' (1980)
Street fighter Eastwood earns a living from bare-knuckle boxing matches. / Als Straßenkämpfer verdient sich Eastwood seinen Lebensunterhalt mit Faustkämpfen. / Eastwood en bagarreur gagnant sa vie dans des combats à mains nues.

2

VISUAL FILMOGRAPHY

FILMOGRAFIE IN BILDERN
FILMOGRAPHIE EN IMAGES

APPRENTICE

LEHRJAHRE

L'APPRENTISSAGE

UNIVERSAL STUDIOS (1956)
Eastwood hears Marlon Brando speak about acting. / Eastwood hört zu, wie Marlon Brando über die Schauspielerei spricht. / Eastwood écoute Marlon Brando parler du métier d'acteur.

PAGE 22
PORTRAIT (CIRCA 1955)
Eastwood at age 25 as a student in Universal's Talent School. / Eastwood im Alter von 25 Jahren an der Talentschule von Universal. / Eastwood à 25 ans, étudiant à l'école d'acteurs des studios Universal.

"I love every aspect of the creation of motion pictures and I guess I am committed to it for life."
Clint Eastwood

UNIVERSAL STUDIOS (1956)
Eastwood bends over Gia Scala during an acting workshop. / Während eines Schauspielseminars beugt sich Eastwood über Gia Scala. / Eastwood penché sur Gia Scala pendant un atelier.

„Ich liebe jeden Aspekt des Filmemachens, und ich schätze, das ist meine Lebensaufgabe."
Clint Eastwood

« J'adore la création cinématographique dans ses moindres aspects et je crois que je ferai ça toute ma vie. »
Clint Eastwood

UNIVERSAL STUDIOS (1956)
Gia Scala and Eastwood take dance lessons. / Gia Scala und Eastwood nehmen Tanzunterricht. / Gia Scala et Eastwood prennent des cours de danse.

"What struck me most about Clint was his indolent way of moving. It seemed to me Clint closely resembled a cat."
Sergio Leone on seeing Clint Eastwood in 'Rawhide'

„Was mich am meisten an Clint faszinierte, war sein schleichender Gang. Mir schien, Clint war einer Katze sehr ähnlich."
Sergio Leone über seinen Eindruck von Clint Eastwood in *Cowboy* (*Tausend Meilen Staub*)

« Ce qui me frappait le plus chez Clint, c'était sa manière indolente de se déplacer. On aurait dit un chat. »
Sergio Leone à propos de Clint Eastwood dans *Rawhide*

UNIVERSAL STUDIOS (1956)
Eastwood joins three budding actresses in body conditioning class. / Eastwood mit weiblichem Schauspielernachwuchs beim Körpertraining. / Cours de gym en compagnie de trois actrices en herbe.

PAGES 28 & 29
PORTRAITS (CIRCA 1956)
Glamour-boy and beefcake shots from Eastwood's early studio days. / Aufnahmen von Eastwood als Glamour-Boy und Muskelprotz in seiner Frühzeit als Vertragsschauspieler. / Eastwood en jeune premier et en bel étalon.

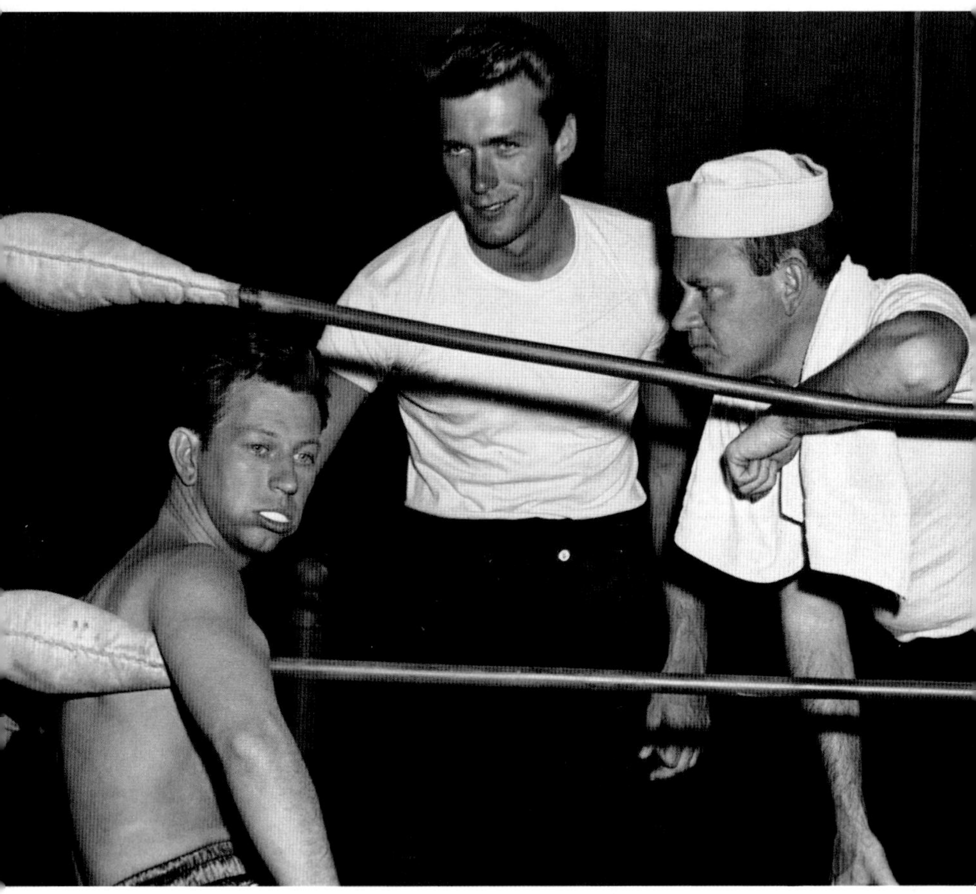

STILL FROM 'FRANCIS IN THE NAVY' (1955)
Appearing in a 'Francis the Talking Mule' movie with Donald O'Connor (seated). / Auftritt mit Donald O'Connor (sitzend) in einem Film über „Francis, das sprechende Maultier". / Avec Donald O'Connor (assis) dans une aventure de « Francis la mule qui parle ».

STILL FROM 'LADY GODIVA OF COVENTRY' (1955)

Eastwood (right) appears in period costume for this medieval drama. / Eastwood (rechts) trägt in dem Mittelalterdrama ein historisches Kostüm. / Eastwood (à droite) en costume d'époque pour un drame médiéval.

PORTRAIT FOR 'THE FIRST TRAVELING SALESLADY' (1956)
Secretary Carol Channing is aggressively wooed by dashing lieutenant Eastwood. / Carol Channing wird als Sekretärin von dem forschen Leutnant (Eastwood) aggressiv umworben. / Le fringant lieutenant (Eastwood) et la jolie secrétaire (Carol Channing).

PAGES 34 & 35
PORTRAITS FOR 'RAWHIDE' (1959–1966)
Eastwood as an amiable, clean-cut cowboy on a cattle drive. / Eastwood als liebenswerter, anständiger Cowboy beim Viehtrieb. / Eastwood en cow-boy aimable et propret.

STILL FROM 'THE FIRST TRAVELING SALESLADY' (1956)
In this Western comedy, Eastwood (right) finds the sheriff tied up. / In dieser Westernkomödie findet Eastwood (rechts) den Sheriff gefesselt vor. / Western comique où Eastwood (à droite) retrouve le shérif ligoté.

WANTED

LBS. NET

PORTRAIT FOR 'RAWHIDE' (1959–1966)
Eastwood would continue his physical fitness regime throughout his life. / Eastwood hielt sich sein Leben lang körperlich fit. / Eastwood continuera toute sa vie à entretenir sa condition physique.

PORTRAIT FOR 'RAWHIDE' (1959–1966)
The muscles that made Eastwood a hero and romantic interest. / Die Muskeln, die Eastwood zum Helden und Frauenliebling machten. / Les muscles qui feront d'Eastwood le héros de ces messieurs et le chouchou de ces dames.

"I've always felt that there are really only two American art forms: jazz and the Western movie."
Clint Eastwood

„Ich hatte schon immer das Gefühl, dass es nur zwei echte amerikanische Kunstformen gibt: Jazz und Westernfilme."
Clint Eastwood

« Il m'a toujours semblé qu'il n'existait que deux formes d'art typiquement américaines : le jazz et le western. »
Clint Eastwood

PORTRAIT (CIRCA 1960)
The TV Western series 'Rawhide' made Eastwood a star. / Durch die Fernsehwesternserie *Cowboys* (*Tausend Meilen Staub*) wurde Eastwood zum Star. / La série télévisée *Rawhide* fait de lui une star.

PAGE 40
POSTER FOR 'A FISTFUL OF DOLLARS' ('PER UN PUGNO DI DOLLARI', 1964)
Three elements that combine to create a Western icon. / Drei Elemente, die zusammen eine Westernikone schufen. / Trois éléments combinés pour créer une légende de l'Ouest.

PAGE 41
STILL FROM 'A FISTFUL OF DOLLARS' (1964)
The Man with No Name (Eastwood) with poncho and Colt .45. / Der „namenlose" Joe (Eastwood) mit Poncho und 45er Colt. / L'Hommme sans nom (Eastwood) avec son poncho et son colt 45.

This short cigar belongs to a man with no name.
This long gun belongs to a man with no name.
This poncho belongs to a man with no name.
He's going to trigger a whole new style in adventure.

STILL FROM 'A FISTFUL OF DOLLARS' (1964)
Eastwood discusses plans with cantina owner and confidant José Calvo. / Eastwood bespricht seine Pläne mit dem Cantina-Wirt und Vertrauten Silvanito (José Calvo). / En grande conversation avec le patron de la cantina (José Calvo).

"You see, my mule don't like people laughing. He gets the crazy idea you're laughing at him. Now if you apologize like I know you're going to, I might convince him that you really didn't mean it."
The Man with No Name (Clint Eastwood)

STILL FROM 'A FISTFUL OF DOLLARS' (1964)
The Man with No Name (Eastwood) helps the coffin-maker's business. / Der „namenlose" Joe (Eastwood) kurbelt die Geschäfte des Sargmachers an. / L'Homme sans nom (Eastwood) fait marcher les affaires du fabricant de cercueils.

„Seht mal, mein Maulesel mag nicht, wenn die Leute lachen. Er hat dann die verrückte Vorstellung, sie lachten über ihn. Wenn ihr euch also jetzt entschuldigt, was ihr mit Sicherheit tun werdet, dann kann ich ihn vielleicht davon überzeugen, dass ihr es wirklich nicht so gemeint habt."
Der „namenlose" Joe (Clint Eastwood)

« Voyez-vous, mon mulet n'aime pas que les gens rient. Il se met dans la tête qu'on se moque de lui. Mais si vous vous excusez, comme je suis sûr que vous allez le faire, j'arriverai peut-être à le convaincre que vous ne le pensiez pas vraiment. »
L'Homme sans nom (Clint Eastwood)

"I also learned from watching the Italians how to make only a few dollars look like twice that much on the screen."
Clint Eastwood

„Als ich den Italienern zuschaute, habe ich auch gelernt, wie man ein paar Dollar auf der Leinwand wie das Doppelte aussehen lässt."
Clint Eastwood

« J'ai aussi appris des Italiens comment faire pour que quelques dollars aient l'air de beaucoup plus à l'écran. »
Clint Eastwood

STILL FROM 'FOR A FEW DOLLARS MORE' ('PER QUALCHE DOLLARO IN PIÙ', 1965)
Bankrobber Gian Maria Volontè has a momentary advantage over Eastwood. / Bankräuber „El Indio" (Gian Maria Volontè) gewinnt kurzfristig die Oberhand über Monco (Eastwood). / El Indio (Gian Maria Volontè) a momentanément l'avantage sur notre héros.

STILL FROM 'FOR A FEW DOLLARS MORE' (1965)
Eastwood carts off the bodies, including villain Gian Maria Volontè. / Monco (Eastwood) schafft die Leichen fort, darunter die des Oberschurken (Gian Maria Volontè). / L'Homme sans nom et sa cargaison de cadavres, dont celui du bandit Gian Maria Volontè.

STILL FROM 'FOR A FEW DOLLARS MORE' (1965)
Three to one, but the odds are in Eastwood's favor! / Drei gegen einen – die Chancen stehen gut für Monco (Eastwood)! / À trois contre un, Eastwood reste favori !

STILL FROM 'THE WITCHES' ('LE STREGHE', 1965)
Bored housewife Silvana Mangano imagines that husband Eastwood still desires her. / Die gelangweilte Hausfrau (Silvana Mangano) stellt sich vor, dass ihr Ehemann (Eastwood) sie noch immer begehrt. / Une ménagère esseulée (Silvana Mangano) rêve d'attiser le désir de son mari (Eastwood).

STILL FROM 'THE WITCHES' (1965)
Eastwood is a violently jealous gunfighter in his wife's sexual fantasy. / In den Sexualphantasien seiner Ehefrau spielt Eastwood einen eifersüchtigen Revolverhelden, der auch vor Gewalt nicht zurückschreckt. / Dans les fantasmes de sa femme, Eastwood est un amant jaloux à la gâchette facile.

STILL FROM 'THE GOOD, THE BAD AND THE UGLY' ('IL BUONO, IL BRUTTO, IL CATTIVO', 1966)

The Good (Eastwood) isn't much better than The Bad (Lee Van Cleef, left). / „Il buono" (der Gute, Eastwood) ist nicht viel besser als „il brutto" (der Böse, Lee Van Cleef, links). / Le Bon (Eastwood) n'est guère meilleur que la Brute (Lee Van Cleef, à gauche).

"In this world, there's two kinds of people, my friend: those with loaded guns and those who dig. You dig!"

The Man with No Name (Clint Eastwood) speaking to Tuco (Eli Wallach)

STILL FROM 'THE GOOD, THE BAD AND THE UGLY' (1966)
Bounty hunter Eastwood and bandit Eli Wallach are distrustful partners. / Kopfgeldjäger Blondie (Eastwood) und Bandit Tuco (Eli Wallach) trauen sich als Partner nicht über den Weg. / Le chasseur de primes (Eastwood) et le Truand (Eli Wallach) en complices méfiants.

„Es gibt zwei Arten von Menschen auf dieser Welt: Die einen haben einen geladenen Revolver und die anderen buddeln. Du buddelst!"
Blondie (Clint Eastwood) zu Tuco (Eli Wallach)

« En ce bas monde, il y a deux sortes de gens, mon ami : ceux qui ont un flingue chargé et ceux qui creusent. Toi, tu creuses ! »
L'Homme sans nom (Clint Eastwood) s'adressant à Tuco (Eli Wallach)

STILL FROM 'THE GOOD, THE BAD AND THE UGLY' (1966)

Eastwood shoots the rope to save Eli Wallach from a hanging. / Blondie (Eastwood) durchschießt den Strick, um Tuco (Eli Wallach) vor dem Galgen zu retten. / Le Bon coupe la corde d'un coup de revolver pour sauver le Truand.

"There are a lot of marvelous actors in the world with better training and schooling than me but if they'd played Dirty Harry it wouldn't suit them. Olivier would have looked ridiculous with a poncho and pistol."
Clint Eastwood

„Es gibt viele großartige Schauspieler auf der Welt, die besser geschult und ausgebildet sind als ich, aber Dirty Harry zu spielen, würde nicht zu ihnen passen. Olivier hätte mit Poncho und Pistole lächerlich ausgesehen."
Clint Eastwood

STILL FROM 'THE GOOD, THE BAD AND THE UGLY' (1966)
Due to his double-crossing partner, Eastwood's neck is in the noose. / Dem falschen Spiel seines Partners hat es Blondie (Eastwood) zu verdanken, das sein Hals in der Schlinge steckt. / Trahi par son acolyte, le Bon se retrouve la corde au cou.

« Il y a beaucoup de merveilleux acteurs dans le monde qui ont une bien meilleure formation que moi mais qui n'auraient pas fait l'affaire pour jouer l'inspecteur Harry. [Laurence] Olivier aurait eu l'air ridicule avec un poncho et un pistolet. »
Clint Eastwood

STILL FROM 'THE GOOD, THE BAD AND THE UGLY' (1966)
A bedroom scene with a prostitute cut from the U.S. release. / Diese Schlafzimmerszene mit einer Prostituierten wurde amerikanischen Kinobesuchern vorenthalten. / Scène érotique avec une prostituée (retirée de la version américaine).

STILL FROM 'THE GOOD, THE BAD AND THE UGLY' (1966)
Graveyard humor as Eastwood has the last laugh at Eli Wallach. / Schwarzer Humor – und Blondie (Eastwood) lacht zuletzt über Tuco (Eli Wallach). / Le Bon et le Truand : rira bien qui rira le dernier.

STILL FROM 'THE GOOD, THE BAD AND THE UGLY' (1966)

Eli Wallach, Eastwood, and Lee Van Cleef in the three-way showdown. / Eli Wallach, Eastwood und Lee Van Cleef im Showdown zu dritt. / Eli Wallach, Eastwood et Lee Van Cleef lors de l'épreuve de force finale.

"I do the kinds of roles I'd like to see if I were still digging swimming pools and wanted to escape my problems."
Clint Eastwood

„Ich spiele die Art von Rollen, die ich mir gerne anschauen würde, wenn ich noch immer Swimmingpools ausheben würde und vor meinen Problemen fliehen wollte."
Clint Eastwood

« Je joue le genre de rôles que j'aimerais voir si je creusais encore des piscines et si je voulais oublier mes soucis. »
Clint Eastwood

STILL FROM 'THE GOOD, THE BAD AND THE UGLY' (1966)

The eyes narrow, the lips snarl, and the teeth clench. / Die Augen zusammengekniffen, die Lippen schmal, die Zähne zusammengebissen. / Yeux plissés, lèvres retroussées, dents serrées.

STILL FROM 'HANG 'EM HIGH' (1968)
Vigilantes humiliate Eastwood by dragging him across the Rio Grande River. / Vigilanten demütigen Jed (Eastwood), indem sie ihn über den Río Grande schleifen. / Humilié par des justiciers qui le traînent dans le Río Grande.

STILL FROM 'HANG 'EM HIGH' (1968)
Eastwood is almost lynched for a murder he didn't commit. / Jed (Eastwood) wird beinahe für einen Mord gelyncht, den er nicht begangen hat. / À deux doigts d'y passer pour un meurtre qu'il n'a pas commis.

DEPUTY

ON THE SET OF 'HANG 'EM HIGH' (1968)
Eastwood brings his "Man with No Name" persona to Hollywood. / Eastwood bringt seine Figur des „Namenlosen" nach Hollywood. / Eastwood alias « l'Homme sans nom » débarque à Hollywood.

"You make two mistakes: you hung the wrong man, and you didn't finish the job."
Jed Cooper (Clint Eastwood)

„Ihr habt zwei Fehler gemacht: Ihr habt den falschen Kerl aufgeknüpft, und ihr habt eure Arbeit nicht zu Ende gebracht."
Jed Cooper (Clint Eastwood)

STILL FROM 'HANG 'EM HIGH' (1968)
Is U.S. Marshal Eastwood out for justice or revenge? / Will US-Marshal Jed Cooper (Eastwood) Rache oder Gerechtigkeit? / Le marshal est-il en quête de justice ou de vengeance ?

« Tu as commis deux erreurs : tu as pendu la mauvaise personne et tu n'as pas fini le boulot. »
Jed Cooper (Clint Eastwood)

STILL FROM 'COOGAN'S BLUFF' (1968)

Eastwood seduces then roughs up drug-dealing hippie Tisha Sterling. / Erst verführt Coogan (Eastwood) Hippiemädchen und Drogendealerin Linny (Tisha Sterling), dann schlägt er sie zusammen. / Le shérif séduit une dealeuse hippie (Tisha Sterling) avant de la malmener.

STILL FROM 'COOGAN'S BLUFF' (1968)

Eastwood in the pool-room fight scene he helped to choreograph. / Eastwood in der Kampfszene im Billardzimmer, deren Choreografie er mitgestaltete. / Scène de bagarre dans une salle de billard chorégraphiée en partie par Eastwood.

PAGES 64/65

ON THE SET OF 'COOGAN'S BLUFF' (1968)

Shooting on a New York street set in Los Angeles as tourists pass by. / Dreharbeiten am New-Yorker-Straßen-Set in Los Angeles, während Touristen vorbeifahren. / Dans une rue de New York recréée à Los Angeles, sous le regard des touristes.

STILL FROM 'WHERE EAGLES DARE' (1968)
Fighting atop a moving cable car suspended above the Austrian Alps. / Kampf auf einer Seilbahn in den österreichischen Alpen. / Bagarre sur le toit d'un téléphérique suspendu au-dessus des Alpes autrichiennes.

PORTRAIT (1968)
Eastwood's first visit to London (to make 'Where Eagles Dare'). / Eastwoods erster Besuch in London (für die Dreharbeiten für *Agenten sterben einsam*). / La première visite d'Eastwood à Londres (pour le tournage de *Quand les aigles attaquent*).

STILL FROM 'PAINT YOUR WAGON' (1969)
With Jean Seberg in a musical Western where Eastwood sings! / Mit Jean Seberg in einem Musical-Western, in dem Eastwood singt! / Avec Jean Seberg dans une comédie musicale où il chante !

STILL FROM 'PAINT YOUR WAGON' (1969)
Jean Seberg, Lee Marvin, and Eastwood in a Western *ménage à trois.* / Jean Seberg, Lee Marvin und Eastwood in einer Western-Dreierbeziehung. / Jean Seberg, Lee Marvin et Eastwood en ménage à trois dans le Far West.

"[Actors like Clint Eastwood have] a kind of dynamic lethargy: they appear to do nothing, and they do everything. They reduce everything to an absolute minimum. For instance, he had perhaps a four-line speech, and he reduced it to four words."
Richard Burton

„[Schauspieler wie Clint Eastwood haben] eine Art dynamischer Lethargie: Sie scheinen nichts zu tun, und sie tun doch alles. Sie reduzieren alles auf ein absolutes Minimum. Wenn er zum Beispiel einen vierzeiligen Text hatte, dann reduzierte er ihn auf vier Worte."
Richard Burton

« [Les acteurs comme Clint Eastwood possèdent] une sorte de léthargie dynamique : ils ont l'air de ne rien faire et ils font tout. Ils réduisent tout au strict minimum. Par exemple, s'il avait une réplique de quatre lignes, il la réduisait à quatre mots. »
Richard Burton

PORTRAIT
Eastwood as the dapper gentleman. / Eastwood als adretter Gentleman. / Eastwood en sémillant gentleman.

FINDING A VOICE

DER RECHTE TON

LE JUSTE TON

PAGE 72

ON THE SET OF 'TWO MULES FOR SISTER SARA' (1970)

Eastwood finds a shady spot to ponder his future career. / Eastwood findet ein schattiges Plätzchen, um über seine berufliche Zukunft nachzudenken. / Eastwood en train de méditer sur sa carrière à l'abri du soleil.

STILL FROM 'TWO MULES FOR SISTER SARA' (1970)

An intimate moment as Shirley MacLaine tends to Eastwood's wound. / Ein Augenblick trauter Zweisamkeit, als sich Sara (Shirley MacLaine) um Hogans (Eastwood) Wunde kümmert. / Moment d'intimité avec Shirley MacLaine qui panse ses plaies.

STILL FROM 'TWO MULES FOR SISTER SARA' (1970)

Eastwood takes a punch from pugilistic nun Shirley MacLaine. / Eastwood muss einen Fausthieb von der kampflustigen Schwester Sara (Shirley MacLaine) einstecken. / Aux prises avec une nonne bagarreuse (Shirley MacLaine).

PAGES 76/77

STILL FROM 'KELLY'S HEROES' (1970)

Eastwood leads his men on a commando raid behind enemy lines. / Der Gefreite Kelly (Eastwood) führt seine Leute in einem Kommandounternehmen hinter feindliche Linien. / À la tête d'une opération commando derrière les lignes ennemies.

STILL FROM 'THE BEGUILED' (1971)
Wounded soldier Eastwood seeks refuge at a school for girls. / Eastwood sucht als verwundeter Soldat Zuflucht in einer Mädchenschule. / Un soldat blessé (Eastwood) trouve refuge dans un pensionnat de jeunes filles.

STILL FROM 'THE BEGUILED' (1971)
Headmistress Géraldine Page provides Eastwood with physical comfort. / Die Schulleiterin (Géraldine Page) sorgt sich um McBurneys (Eastwood) körperliches Wohl. / Réconforté par la directrice (Géraldine Page).

STILL FROM 'THE BEGUILED' (1971)
All the girls, including Jo Ann Harris, seduce and are seduced by Eastwood. / Sämtliche Mädchen, darunter auch Carol (Jo Ann Harris), verführen McBurney (Eastwood) und werden von ihm verführt. / Toutes les filles, y compris Jo Ann Harris, se prêtent au jeu de la séduction.

"Maybe ['The Beguiled'] couldn't have been successful, because the hero failed."
Clint Eastwood

„Vielleicht konnte [Betrogen] gar keinen Erfolg haben, weil der Held versagt."
Clint Eastwood

« Peut-être [Les Proies] ne pouvait-il pas avoir de succès, puisque le héros perdait à la fin. »
Clint Eastwood

STILL FROM 'THE BEGUILED' (1971)
The jealous girls amputate Eastwood's leg as punishment for his philandering. / Die eifersüchtigen Mädchen amputieren McBurneys (Eastwood) Bein als Strafe für seine Flirts. / Les pensionnaires se vengent du coureur de jupons en l'amputant d'une jambe.

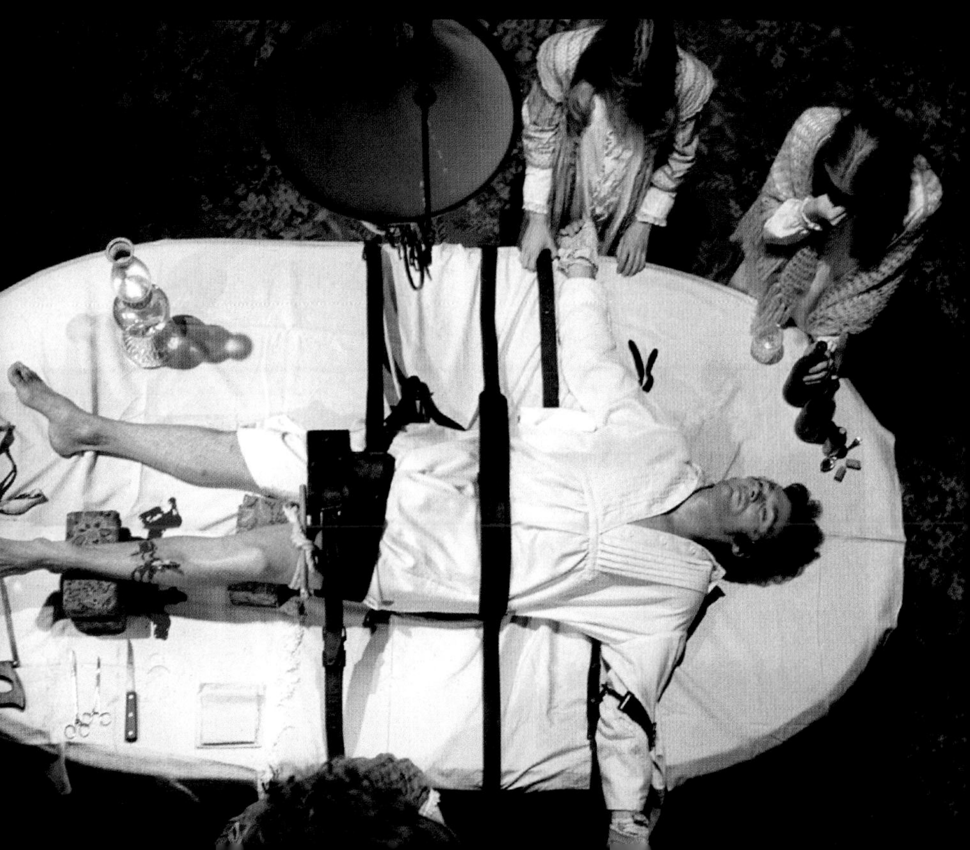

STILL FROM 'PLAY MISTY FOR ME' (1971)
Mentor Don Siegel helps by playing the bartender in Eastwood's directorial debut. / Mentor Don Siegel hilft, indem er den Barmann in Eastwoods Regiedebüt mimt. / Dans le premier film réalisé par Eastwood, son mentor Don Siegel interprète un barman.

STILL FROM 'PLAY MISTY FOR ME' (1971)
Fatally attracted Jessica Walter clings to Eastwood after a one-night stand. / Nach einem One-Night-Stand fühlt sich Evelyn (Jessica Walter) auf verhängnisvolle Weise zu Dave (Eastwood) hingezogen. / Une femme déséquilibrée (Jessica Walter) le harcèle après une liaison sans lendemain.

"There's only one problem with this film, Clint: it doesn't have Hitchcock's name on it."
John Cassavetes

„Es gibt mit diesem Film nur ein Problem, Clint: Es steht nicht der Name Hitchcock drauf."
John Cassavetes

« Ce film n'a qu'un défaut, Clint : il n'y a pas le nom de Hitchcock écrit dessus. »
John Cassavetes

STILL FROM 'PLAY MISTY FOR ME' (1971)
Eastwood is attacked by crazed fan Jessica Walter. / Dave (Eastwood) wird von seinem durchgedrehten Fan (Jessica Walter) angegriffen. / Aux prises avec son admiratrice enragée (Jessica Walter).

STILL FROM 'PLAY MISTY FOR ME' (1971)
Clarice Taylor feels the stabs of Jessica Walter's jealousy. / Birdie (Clarice Taylor) bekommt die stechende Eifersucht von Evelyn (Jessica Walter) zu spüren. / Birdie (Clarice Taylor) victime de la jalousie d'Evelyn (Jessica Walter).

STILL FROM 'DIRTY HARRY' (1971)
Psycho killer Andy Robinson takes aim at helplessly liberal San Francisco. / Der Psychokiller (Andy Robinson) nimmt das hilflos ausgelieferte liberale San Francisco ins Visier. / Un tueur psychopathe (Andy Robinson) pointe son viseur sur la population de San Francisco, cible facile dans une ville excessivement ouverte et libérale.

"Nothing wrong with shooting so long as the right people get shot."
Harry Callahan (Clint Eastwood)

„Schießen ist in Ordnung, solange die richtigen Leute erschossen werden."
Harry Callahan (Clint Eastwood)

« Il n'y a rien de mal à tirer des coups de revolver du moment que ce sont les bonnes personnes qui les reçoivent. »
Harry Callahan (Clint Eastwood)

STILL FROM 'DIRTY HARRY' (1971)
Only Eastwood stands between the killer and his potential victims. / Nur Harry (Eastwood) steht zwischen dem Killer und seinen potentiellen Opfern. / Seul Harry se dresse entre le tueur et ses victimes potentielles.

STILL FROM 'DIRTY HARRY' (1971)
Masked madman Andy Robinson gives Eastwood a brutal kicking. / Der maskierte Geisteskranke (Andy Robinson) gibt Harry (Eastwood) einen brutalen Tritt. / Le tueur masqué (Andy Robinson) passe un savon à Harry.

STILL FROM 'DIRTY HARRY' (1971)
Eastwood extracts information by stepping on Andy Robinson's wounded leg. / Eastwood verschafft sich Informationen, indem er sich auf das verletzte Bein des Mörders (Andy Robinson) stellt. / Harry soutire des informations au tueur (Andy Robinson) en appuyant sur sa jambe blessée.

PAGES 90 & 91
ON THE SET OF 'DIRTY HARRY' (1971)
Eastwood performed this stunt jump onto a moving bus. / Eastwood sprang bei diesem Stunt selbst auf den fahrenden Bus. / Eastwood réalise lui-même cette cascade sur un bus en marche.

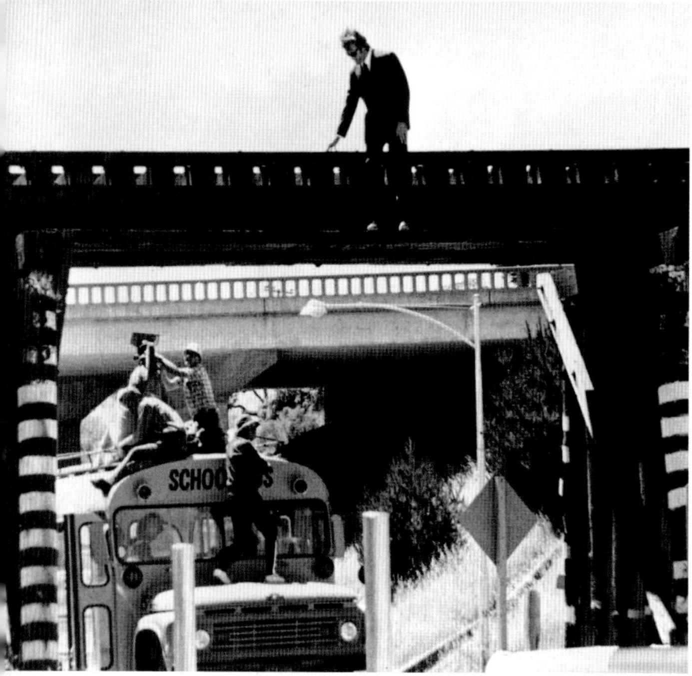

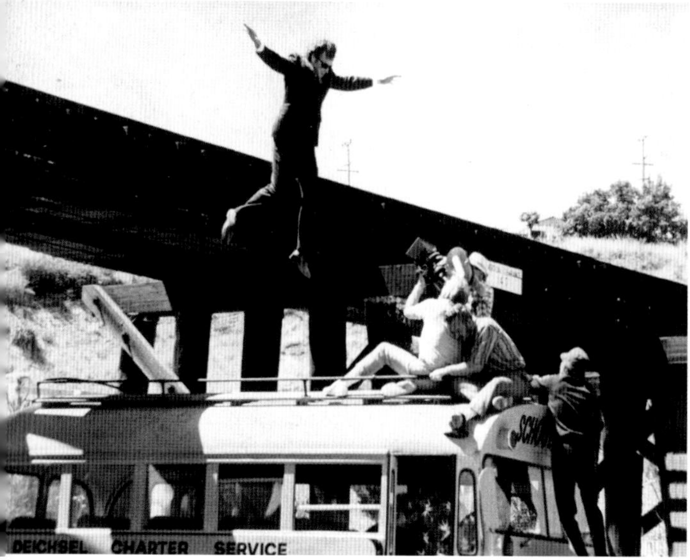
DEICHSEL CHARTER SERVICE

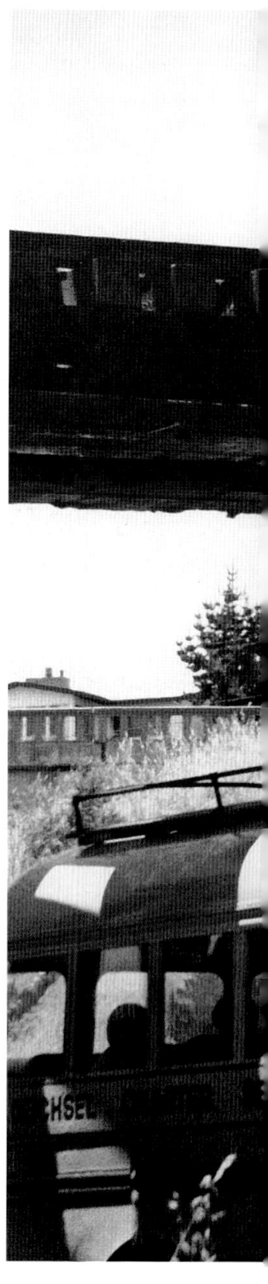

SCHOOL BUS
KEEP

STILL FROM 'JOE KIDD' (1972)
Joe Kidd (Eastwood) is caught napping, but he's awake now! / Joe Kidd (Eastwood) hat man beim Nickerchen erwischt – aber jetzt ist er hellwach! / Joe Kidd (Eastwood) surpris en pleine sieste.

PAGES 92/93
STILL FROM 'DIRTY HARRY' (1971)
Who will stop you? "Smith and Wesson – and me." / Wer kann euch aufhalten? „Smith und Wesson – und ich." / Qui vous arrêtera ? « Smith & Wesson… et moi. »

STILL FROM 'JOE KIDD' (1972)
Drunken Eastwood sobers up to fight a greedy land baron. / Der betrunkene Joe (Eastwood) will schnell nüchtern werden, um gegen den habgierigen Großgrundbesitzer zu kämpfen. / Il dessoûlera vite pour combattre un infâme propriétaire terrien.

"Someone asked why I like shooting on location as opposed to in the studio. I said, 'In the studio, everyone's looking around for a chair. On location, everyone's working.'"
Clint Eastwood

„Es hat mich mal jemand gefragt, warum ich gerne draußen filme und nicht im Studio. Ich habe geantwortet: ‚Im Studio sucht jeder nach einem Stuhl, wo er sich hinsetzen kann. Draußen arbeiten alle.'"
Clint Eastwood

« Quelqu'un m'a demandé pourquoi je préférais tourner en extérieurs plutôt qu'en studio. J'ai répondu : "En studio, tout le monde cherche une chaise. En extérieur, tout le monde bosse." »
Clint Eastwood

STILL FROM 'HIGH PLAINS DRIFTER' (1973)
The Stranger (Eastwood) rides into town like an avenging angel. / „Der Fremde" (Eastwood) reitet wie ein Racheengel in die Stadt ein. / L'Étranger (Eastwood) arrive en ville tel un ange vengeur.

"Although friendly enough to Mexicans, Indians, and the midget, vengeful, contemptuous Eastwood is a cruel hero in a corrupt, degenerate, cowardly civilization."
J. Hoberman

„Obwohl er sich Mexikanern, Indianern und dem Zwerg gegenüber einigermaßen freundlich gibt, ist der rachsüchtige, verächtliche Eastwood ein grausamer Held in einer korrupten, degenerierten, feigen Zivilisation."
J. Hoberman

STILL FROM 'HIGH PLAINS DRIFTER' (1973)
Eastwood will make dwarf Billy Curtis both town sheriff and mayor. / „Der Fremde" (Eastwood) möchte den kleinwüchsigen Mordecai (Billy Curtis) sowohl zum Sheriff als auch zum Bürgermeister der Stadt machen. / L'Étranger fera du nain (Billy Curtis) le shérif et le maire de la ville.

« Bien qu'assez amical envers les Mexicains, les Indiens et le nain, Eastwood est un héros cruel, vengeur et méprisant dans une civilisation corrompue, dégénérée et lâche. »
J. Hoberman

PANASPEED MOTOR
VARIABLE CONTROL
R-200°

STILL FROM 'BREEZY' (1973)
Cynical businessman William Holden rediscovers life through hippie Kay Lenz. / Der zynische Geschäftsmann Frank Harmon (William Holden) entdeckt durch Hippie „Breezy" (Kay Lenz) das Leben neu. / Un homme d'affaires cynique (William Holden) redécouvre la vie grâce à une hippie (Kay Lenz).

ON THE SET OF 'BREEZY' (1973)
Eastwood directs William Holden and Kay Lenz in this May-December romance. / Eastwood gibt William Holden und Kay Lenz Regieanweisungen in der „Romanze zwischen Lenz und Lebensabend". / Eastwood dirige une histoire d'amour entre un homme mûr (William Holden) et une jeune femme (Kay Lenz).

"She sees and feels what he's stopped seeing and feeling, all those things in life that he doesn't take the time to enjoy."
Clint Eastwood on Breezy (Kay Lenz)

„Sie sieht und fühlt, was er nicht mehr sieht und fühlt, all diese Dinge im Leben, für die er sich nicht die Zeit nimmt, sie zu genießen."
Clint Eastwood über Breezy (Kay Lenz)

« Elle voit et elle ressent ce qu'il a cessé de voir et de ressentir, toutes les choses dans la vie qu'il ne prend pas le temps de savourer. »
Clint Eastwood à propos de Breezy (Kay Lenz)

STILL FROM 'MAGNUM FORCE' (1973)
Dirty Harry (Eastwood) is temporarily downed by even dirtier (corrupt) cops. / Der „schmutzige" Harry (Eastwood) wird von noch „schmutzigeren" (korrupten) Polizisten vorübergehend außer Gefecht gesetzt. / L'inspecteur Harry (Eastwood) est mis momentanément neutralisé par des collègues encore moins scrupuleux que lui.

"If crime were caused by super-evil dragons, there would be no Miranda, no Escobedo; we could all be licensed to kill, like Dirty Harry. But since crime is caused by deprivation, misery, psychopathology, and social injustice, 'Dirty Harry' is a deeply immoral movie."
Pauline Kael

„Wenn ganz böse Drachen die Ursache des Verbrechens wären, dann brauchten wir keine verfassungsmäßigen Rechte für Beschuldigte; wir könnten alle die Genehmigung zum Töten erhalten, wie Dirty Harry. Weil aber Armut, Elend, Geisteskrankheit und soziale Ungerechtigkeit die Ursachen für Verbrechen sind, ist Dirty Harry *ein zutiefst unmoralischer Film."*
Pauline Kael

« Si la délinquance était provoquée par des dragons maléfiques, il n'y aurait pas de droits de la défense ; nous serions tous autorisés à tuer, comme l'inspecteur Harry. Mais sachant que la délinquance est engendrée par la privation, la misère, les psychopathologies et l'injustice sociale, L'Inspecteur Harry *est un film profondément immoral. »*
Pauline Kael

STILL FROM 'MAGNUM FORCE' (1973)
Eastwood sends bad cop David Soul flying into San Francisco Bay. / Eastwood schickt den korrupten Polizisten Davis (David Soul) in hohem Bogen in die Bucht von San Francisco. / Harry expédie un flic ripou (David Soul) dans la baie de San Francisco.

STILL FROM 'THUNDERBOLT AND LIGHTFOOT' (1974)
Eastwood is a bank robber under the phony preacher disguise. / Eastwood spielt einen als Prediger verkleideten Bankräuber. / Un braqueur de banques déguisé en pasteur.

STILL FROM 'THUNDERBOLT AND LIGHTFOOT' (1974)
Eastwood with partner-in-crime Jeff Bridges in drag disguise. / „Thunderbolt" (Eastwood) und sein Komplize (Jeff Bridges), als Frau verkleidet. / Thunderbolt et son complice (Jeff Bridges) travesti en femme.

PAGE 104
STILL FROM 'THE EIGER SANCTION' (1975)
Eastwood on top of the Totem Pole in Monument Valley. / Eastwood auf dem „Totempfahl" im Monument Valley. / Au sommet du Totem Pole, dans la Monument Valley.

PAGE 105
STILL FROM 'THE EIGER SANCTION' (1975)
Eastwood hanging from the Eiger Mountain in the Swiss Alps. / Eastwood hängt am Eiger in den Schweizer Alpen. / Suspendu aux parois de l'Eiger dans les Alpes suisses.

ON THE SET OF 'THE EIGER SANCTION' (1975)
George Kennedy watches Eastwood commune with a cow. / George Kennedy schaut zu, wie sich Eastwood mit einer Kuh unterhält. / Communion avec une vache sous le regard amusé de George Kennedy.

ON THE SET OF 'THE EIGER SANCTION' (1975)
Eastwood films a hanging stunt on location in Zurich. / Eastwood bei Außenaufnahmen zu einem Hängestunt in Zürich. / Eastwood filme une cascade à Zurich.

STILL FROM 'THE OUTLAW JOSEY WALES' (1976)

Sondra Locke offers Eastwood new love after his wife is massacred. / Nach dem Massaker an seiner Frau findet Josey (Eastwood) in Laura Lee (Sondra Locke) eine neue Liebe. / Après le massacre de sa femme, il retrouve l'amour auprès de Laura (Sondra Locke).

Josey Wales (Clint Eastwood): *"Whenever I get to likin'someone, they aren't around long."*
Lone Watie (Chief Dan George): *"I notice when you get to dislikin'someone, they ain't around for long neither."*

STILL FROM 'THE OUTLAW JOSEY WALES' (1976)
Eastwood engages in a "blood brother" handclasp with Indian Will Sampson. / Josey (Eastwood) bei einem „blutsbrüderlichen" Handschlag mit dem Indianer Ten Bears (Will Sampson). / Pacte du sang avec l'Indien Will Sampson.

Josey Wales (Clint Eastwood): *„Immer wenn ich anfange, jemanden zu mögen, bleibt er nicht lange."*
Lone Watie (Häuptling Dan George): *„Mir ist aufgefallen, wenn du jemanden nicht magst, dann bleibt er auch nicht lange."*

Josey Wales (Clint Eastwood). – *À chaque fois qu'une personne me plaît, elle ne fait pas long feu.*
Lone Watie (Chef Dan George). – *J'ai remarqué que quand une personne ne vous plaît pas, elle ne fait pas long feu non plus.*

STILL FROM 'THE OUTLAW JOSEY WALES' (1976)
Eastwood impales murderous soldier Bill McKinney on his own sword. / Josey (Eastwood) spießt den Mordbrenner Terrill (Bill McKinney) auf seiner eigenen Stichwaffe auf. / Il empale un soldat (Bill McKinney) sur sa propre épée.

STILL FROM 'THE OUTLAW JOSEY WALES' (1976)
"Are you gonna pull those pistols or whistle Dixie?" / „Ziehst du jetzt oder pfeifst du Dixie?" / « Tu vas les sortir, ces flingues, ou tu vas nous siffler Dixie ? »

"I guess we all died in a little in that damn war."
Josey Wales (Clint Eastwood) on the U.S. Civil War (and Vietnam?)

„Ich schätze, in diesem verdammten Krieg sind wir alle ein bisschen gestorben."
Josey Wales (Clint Eastwood) über den amerikanischen Sezessionskrieg (und Vietnam?)

« Je crois que nous somme tous un peu morts pendant cette maudite guerre. »
Josey Wales (Clint Eastwood) à propos de la guerre de Sécession (et du Viêtnam ?)

GROCERIES

STILL FROM 'THE ENFORCER' (1976)
Eastwood's bazooka blast takes out the terrorist in the watchtower. / Mit einer Panzerfaust schaltet Harry (Eastwood) die Terroristen auf dem Wachturm aus. / Coup de bazooka sur la tour de guet abritant un terroriste.

STILL FROM 'THE ENFORCER' (1976)
Eastwood about to exchange gunfire in the rooftop chase scene. / Harry (Eastwood) kurz vor dem Schusswechsel während der Verfolgungsjagd über die Dächer. / Prêt à tirer lors d'une poursuite sur les toits.

"Dirty Harry burst out of the darkness at a time when cops were being celebrated as heroes and vilified as pigs and somehow managed to be both."
J. Hoberman

„Dirty Harry tauchte auf in einer Zeit, in der Polizisten als Helden gefeiert und als Bullen verunglimpft wurden und es irgendwie schafften, beides zu sein."
J. Hoberman

« L'inspecteur Harry a surgi de l'ombre à une époque où les flics étaient fêtés comme des héros et considérés comme des porcs, et il a réussi à être les deux à la fois. »
J. Hoberman

ACTION/REACTION

AKTION/REAKTION

ACTION-RÉACTION

PAGE 114

STILL FROM 'BRONCO BILLY' (1980)

Eastwood as an ex-shoe salesman turned "fastest gun in the West." / Eastwood spielt einen ehemaligen Schuhverkäufer, der zum „schnellsten Schützen im Westen" wurde. / Un ancien marchand de chaussures reconverti en « meilleur tireur de l'Ouest ».

ON THE SET OF 'THE GAUNTLET' (1977)

Eastwood directs co-star Sondra Locke, his companion for thirteen years. / Eastwood gibt seiner Kollegin Sondra Locke, mit der er 13 Jahre lang liiert war, Regieanweisungen. / Eastwood dirige Sondra Locke, sa compagne pendant treize ans.

ON THE SET OF 'THE GAUNTLET' (1977)

Eastwood and Sondra Locke travel by foot, car, train, bus – and motorcycle. / Ben (Eastwood) und Gus (Sondra Locke) reisen zu Fuß, mit dem Auto, dem Zug, dem Bus – und dem Motorrad. / Eastwood et Sondra Locke voyagent à pied, en voiture, en train, en bus... et en moto.

STILL FROM 'EVERY WHICH WAY BUT LOOSE' (1978)
Eastwood's beer buddy Clyde is "a very natural method actor." / Philos (Eastwood) Saufkumpan Clyde ist eine Naturbegabung. / Clyde, son compagnon de beuverie, est « un acteur né ».

"The orangutan took a liking to Clint. It was a little scary sometimes. He'd put his arms around Clint and play with his Adam's apple."
Buddy Van Horn

„Der Orang-Utan mochte Clint. Manchmal war es schon beängstigend. Er legte seine Arme um Clint und begann, mit seinem Adamsapfel zu spielen."
Buddy Van Horn

ON THE SET OF 'EVERY WHICH WAY BUT LOOSE' (1978)
Rehearsing with director James Fargo and the orangutan's human double. / Probedurchlauf mit Regisseur James Fargo und dem menschlichen Double des Orang-Utans. / Répétition avec le réalisateur James Fargo et le double humain de l'orang-outan.

« L'orang-outan s'est pris d'affection pour Clint. C'était un peu inquiétant par moments. Il prenait Clint dans ses bras et jouait avec sa pomme d'Adam. »
Buddy Van Horn

SP
PACIFIC

STILL FROM 'ESCAPE FROM ALCATRAZ' (1979)
Bruce M. Fischer attempts to knife Eastwood in the prison courtyard. / Wolf (Bruce M. Fischer) versucht, Morris (Eastwood) im Gefängnishof abzustechen. / Un détenu (Bruce M. Fischer) tente de le poignarder dans la cour de la prison.

STILL FROM 'ESCAPE FROM ALCATRAZ' (1979)
Other inmates taunt Eastwood as he arrives at Alcatraz prison. / Bei seiner Ankunft wird Morris (Eastwood) von anderen Häftlingen verspottet. / À son arrivée à la prison d'Alcatraz, il se fait railler par ses codétenus.

STILL FROM 'BRONCO BILLY' (1980)
Eastwood performs shooting stunts as star of a Wild West show. / Als Star einer Wildwestshow zeigt Billy (Eastwood) seine Schießkunst. / Star d'un spectacle western, Bronco Billy (Eastwood) exécute des numéros de tir.

"Every picture takes on its own style. I get into the film and then I get the look of it as it comes, rather than having a constant style that goes through each film."
Clint Eastwood

„Jeder Film hat seinen eigenen Stil. Ich gehe an den Film heran und bekomme das, was dabei herauskommt, statt eines konstanten Stils, den man in jedem meiner Filme wiederfindet."
Clint Eastwood

STILL FROM 'BRONCO BILLY' (1980)
Sondra Locke tied to the "wheel of fortune" for the knife-throwing act. / Für die Messerwerfernummer wird Antoinette (Sondra Locke) am „Glücksrad" festgebunden. / Sondra Locke ligotée à la « roue de la fortune » pour le lancer de couteau.

STILL FROM 'ANY WHICH WAY YOU CAN' (1980)

Monkey see, monkey do: Eastwood mimics the orangutan's mating ritual. / Affentheater: Eastwood ahmt das Paarungsritual des Orang-Utans nach. / Eastwood imitant la parade amoureuse de l'orang-outan.

STILL FROM 'ANY WHICH WAY YOU CAN' (1980)

Clyde the orangutan wants to join Sondra Locke and Eastwood. / Orang-Utan Clyde möchte Lynn (Sondra Locke) und Philo (Eastwood) Gesellschaft leisten. / Clyde, l'orang-outan, veut se joindre à Eastwood et à Sondra Locke.

STILL FROM 'FIREFOX' (1982)
Eastwood as a spy in disguise in this espionage thriller. / Eastwood spielt in diesem Spionagethriller einen verkleideten Spion. / Eastwood voyage incognito pour une mission d'espionnage à haut risque.

STILL FROM 'FIREFOX' (1982)
Eastwood pilots the fighter jet Firefox in aerial combat. / Gant (Eastwood) fliegt den Kampfjet „Firefox" im Luftkampf. / Eastwood aux commandes du Firefox dans un combat aérien.

STILL FROM 'HONKYTONK MAN' (1982)
Eastwood as a country singer journeying across Depression-era America. / Eastwood spielt einen Countrysänger, der durch das Amerika der großen Wirtschaftskrise tingelt. / Eastwood en chanteur de country sillonnant l'Amérique pendant la crise de 29.

"He's a collage. A mixture of Hank Williams, Red Foley, Bob Wills, all those country singers who drank their whiskey neat, burned up their life on the road and ended up by self-destructing."
Clint Eastwood on his character Red Stovall

„Er ist eine Collage, eine Mischung aus Hank Williams, Red Foley, Bob Wills, all diese Countrysänger, die ihren Whiskey pur tranken, ihr Leben auf Tour verheizten und sich am Ende selbst zerstörten."
Clint Eastwood über seine Figur Red Stovall

« C'est un collage. Un mélange de Hank Williams, de Red Foley, de Bob Wills, de tous ces chanteurs de country qui buvaient le whisky sec, consumaient leur existence sur les routes et finissaient par s'autodétruire. »
Clint Eastwood à propos du personnage de Red Stovall

STILL FROM 'HONKYTONK MAN' (1982)
Eastwood's real-life son Kyle, age 14, co-stars with his father. / Eastwoods leiblicher Sohn Kyle, damals 14, spielte hier an der Seite seines Vaters. / Kyle Eastwood jouant aux côtés de son père à l'âge de 14 ans.

PAGE 130
STILL FROM 'SUDDEN IMPACT' (1983)
Dirty Harry (Eastwood) and his .44 Magnum gunning for boardwalk rapists. / Dirty Harry (Eastwood) und seine 44er Magnum warten auf die Vergewaltiger. / L'inspecteur Harry (Eastwood) et son 44 Magnum traquent les violeurs.

PAGE 131
STILLS FROM 'CITY HEAT' (1984)
Eastwood and rival superstar Burt Reynolds ruled Hollywood during this period. / Eastwood und Superstarrivale Burt Reynolds waren damals die größten Zugnummern in Hollywood. / Eastwood et son rival Burt Reynolds tiennent le haut du pavé à Hollywood.

STILL FROM 'TIGHTROPE' (1984)
Does cop Eastwood have the same kinky desires as the sex killer? / Hat der Polizist (Eastwood) die gleichen perversen Gelüste wie der Triebmörder? / Le flic (Eastwood) aurait-il les mêmes penchants pervers que le maniaque sexuel ?

STILL FROM 'TIGHTROPE' (1984)
Eastwood and his detective partner Dan Hedaya uncover a new victim. / Der Polizist Block (Eastwood) und sein Kollege Molinari (Dan Hedaya) entdecken ein neues Opfer. / Les deux policiers (Eastwood et Dan Hedaya) découvrent une nouvelle victime.

„Ich habe am Anfang sogar den Text des Schauspielers nachsynchronisiert, der den Mörder spielte, obwohl ich die Stimme leicht veränderte. Ich wollte nur etwas von einem ‚Ist das Eastwood? Ist er das?'"
Clint Eastwood

"I even looped the lines of the actor who played the killer at the beginning, though I changed the voice slightly. I just wanted a little bit of the thing, 'Is that Eastwood? Is that him?'"
Clint Eastwood

« J'ai même doublé les répliques de l'acteur qui jouait le tueur au début, en changeant un peu ma voix. Je voulais seulement qu'on se demande : "Est-ce que c'est Clint Eastwood ? Est-ce bien lui ?" »
Clint Eastwood

"I think I learned more about direction from [Don Siegel] than from anybody else ... He shoots lean, and he shoots what he wants. He knew when he had it, and he didn't need to cover his ass with a dozen different angles."
Clint Eastwood

„Ich glaube, ich habe von [Don Siegel] mehr über Regie gelernt als von irgendjemand anderem ... Er filmt das, was er haben will, ohne Film zu verschwenden. Er wusste, wann er es im Kasten hatte, und er musste sich nicht mit einem Dutzend Aufnahmen aus anderen Kamerawinkeln absichern."
Clint Eastwood

« Je crois que j'ai plus appris de [Don Siegel] que de n'importe qui en matière de tournage... Il filme le nécessaire, rien que le nécessaire. Il sait quand il a obtenu ce qu'il voulait et il n'a pas besoin de couvrir ses arrières en prenant une dizaine d'angles différents. »
Clint Eastwood

STILL FROM 'PALE RIDER' (1985)
Eastwood returns attempted-rape survivor Sydney Penny to her mother. / Der Prediger bringt Megan (Sydney Penny), die beinah vergewaltigt worden wäre, zu ihrer Mutter zurück. / Le cavalier solitaire ramène la victime d'une tentative de viol (Sydney Penny) auprès de sa mère.

STILL FROM 'HEARTBREAK RIDGE' (1986)
Eastwood whipping his platoon into shape during basic training. / In der Grundausbildung bringt „Gunny" (Eastwood) seinen Zug auf Vordermann. / Eastwood mène la vie dure à ses hommes pendant l'entraînement.

STILL FROM 'HEARTBREAK RIDGE' (1986)
Eastwood in camouflage and battle gear as a macho Marine. / Eastwood in Tarnanzug und Kampfausrüstung als Macho-Marineinfanterist. / En vétéran des Marines vêtu d'une tenue de camouflage.

„Mich hat schon immer interessiert, was Krieger machen, wenn sie keinen Krieg haben."
Clint Eastwood

"What warriors do when they haven't got a war has always interested me."
Clint Eastwood

« Je me suis toujours intéressé à ce que font les guerriers quand il n'y a pas de guerre. »
Clint Eastwood

STILL FROM 'BIRD' (1988)
A jazz movie lit like an old black-and-white photograph in 'Downbeat' magazine. / Ein Jazzfilm, der wie ein altes Schwarzweißfoto in der Zeitschrift *Downbeat* ausgeleuchtet ist. / Un hommage au jazz éclairé comme une vieille photo en noir et blanc dans le magazine *Downbeat*.

"It seems odd, doesn't it, that this Western guy is in love with the blues, and the feeling of pain in those songs, and jazz, but that feeds his soul as well."
Eli Wallach on Clint Eastwood

„Es scheint schon komisch, nicht wahr, dass dieser Westerntyp den Blues mag und das Gefühl des Schmerzes in diesen Liedern und den Jazz, aber das ist auch Futter für seine Seele."
Eli Wallach über Clint Eastwood

« Cela paraît étrange, n'est-ce pas, que cet amateur de westerns ait la passion du blues, de la sensation de douleur qui se dégage de ces chansons, tout comme du jazz ; pourtant, son âme se nourrit aussi de cela. »
Eli Wallach à propos de Clint Eastwood

STILL FROM 'BIRD' (1988)
Jazz saxophonist Charlie Parker (Forest Whitaker) receives accolades. / Jazzsaxophonist Charlie Parker (Forest Whitaker) wird gefeiert. / Le saxophoniste Charlie Parker (Forest Whitaker) acclamé par la foule.

STILL FROM 'THE DEAD POOL' (1988)
Dirty Harry (Eastwood) makes a statement about intrusive TV coverage. / Dirty Harry (Eastwood) gibt deutlich zu verstehen, was er von aufdringlichen Fernsehreportern hält. / L'inspecteur Harry (Eastwood) montre tout le bien qu'il pense des journalistes.

STILL FROM 'PINK CADILLAC' (1989)
Bounty hunter Eastwood tracks down Bernadette Peters at a casino. / Der Kopfgeldjäger (Eastwood) spürt Lou Ann (Bernadette Peters) in einem Spielkasino auf. / Le chasseur de primes (Eastwood) retrouve la fugitive (Bernadette Peters) dans un casino.

"You have to have the picture there in your mind before you make it. And if you don't, you're not a director, you're a guesser."
Clint Eastwood

„Man muss den Film im Kopf haben, bevor man ihn macht. Wenn man das nicht hat, führt man nicht Regie, sondern peilt über den Daumen."
Clint Eastwood

« Vous devez avoir le film clairement en tête avant de commencer. Si ce n'est pas le cas, vous n'êtes pas cinéaste, vous êtes devin. »
Clint Eastwood

STILL FROM 'WHITE HUNTER, BLACK HEART' (1990)

Director John Wilson (Eastwood) would rather shoot an elephant than his film. / Regisseur John Wilson (Eastwood) würde lieber einen Elefanten schießen, statt den Film zu drehen. / Le réalisateur John Wilson (Eastwood), plus intéressé par la chasse que par le tournage de son film.

STILL FROM 'WHITE HUNTER, BLACK HEART' (1990)
Katharine Hepburn (Marisa Berenson) and Humphrey Bogart (Richard Vanstone) lookalikes. / Doppelgänger von Katharine Hepburn (Marisa Berenson) und Humphrey Bogart (Richard Vanstone). / Marisa Berenson et Richard Vanstone en doublures de Katharine Hepburn et de Humphrey Bogart.

"I constantly quote John Wilson, my character in 'White Hunter, Black Heart,' who says 'You can't let eight million popcorn eaters pull you this way or that.'"
Clint Eastwood

„Ich zitiere ständig John Wilson, meine Figur in Weißer Jäger, schwarzes Herz, *der sagt: ‚Man kann sich nicht von acht Millionen Popcornfressern in diese oder jene Richtung drängen lassen.'"*
Clint Eastwood

« Je cite constamment John Wilson, mon personnage dans Chasseur blanc, cœur noir, *qui dit "Vous ne pouvez pas laisser huit millions de bouffeurs de pop-corn vous mener par le bout du nez." »*
Clint Eastwood

STILL FROM 'THE ROOKIE' (1990)

Car thief Raul Julia tries to dominate police detective Eastwood. / Autodieb Strom (Raul Julia) versucht, den Polizisten Pulovski (Eastwood) unter Kontrolle zu bringen. / Le voleur de voitures (Raul Julia) tente de neutraliser le policier (Eastwood).

"There's got to be a hundred reasons why I shouldn't blow you away. But right now I can't think of one."

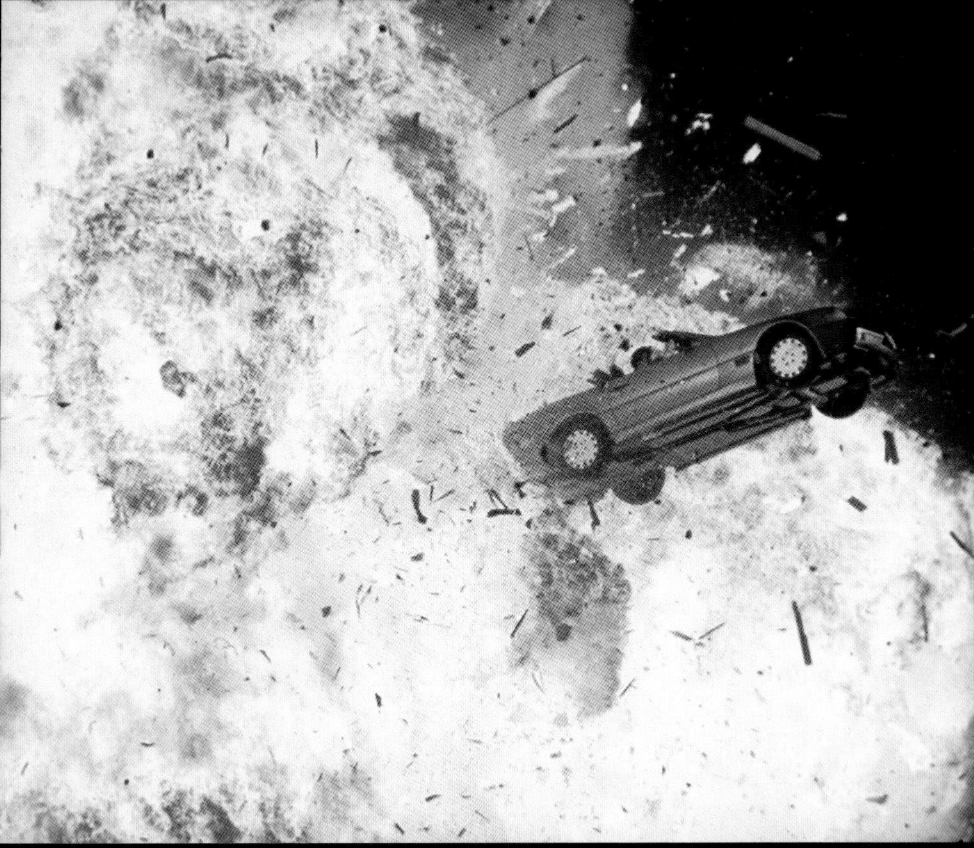

STILL FROM 'THE ROOKIE' (1990)
Eastwood and Charlie Sheen drive like crazy to avoid an explosion. / Pulovski (Eastwood) und Ackerman (Charlie Sheen) fahren wie die Wilden, um der Explosion zu entgehen. / Eastwood et Charlie Sheen échappent de justesse à l'explosion.

PAGE 146
STILLS FROM 'UNFORGIVEN' (1992)
Morgan Freeman is tortured to death by sadistic sheriff Gene Hackman. / Ned Logan (Morgan Freeman) wird von dem sadistischen Sheriff (Gene Hackman) zu Tode gefoltert. / Ned (Morgan Freeman) est torturé à mort par un shérif sadique (Gene Hackman).

PAGE 147
POSTER FOR 'UNFORGIVEN' (1992)
Eastwood as a reformed killer who ends up taking bloody revenge. / Eastwood spielt einen bekehrten Mörder, der am Ende blutige Rache nimmt. / Eastwood en tueur repenti qui finira par céder à la soif de vengeance.

UNFORGIVEN

MAKING PEACE

FRIEDENS-SCHLUSS

LA SÉRÉNITÉ

STILL FROM 'IN THE LINE OF FIRE' (1993)
Guilt-stricken Secret Service agent Eastwood tries to protect the President. / Als von Schuldgefühlen geplagter Agent versucht Eastwood, den Präsidenten zu schützen. / Rongé par les remords, le garde du corps (Eastwood) tente de protéger le nouveau Président.

PAGE 148
STILL FROM 'IN THE LINE OF FIRE' (1993)

"I'm not doing penance for all the characters in action films I've portrayed up till now. But I've reached a stage of my life, we've reached a stage of our history where I said to myself that violence shouldn't be a source of humor or attraction."
Clint Eastwood

„Ich streue mir jetzt keine Asche aufs Haupt für all die Charaktere, die ich bis jetzt in Actionfilmen dargestellt habe. Aber ich habe ein Stadium in meinem Leben erreicht – wir haben ein Stadium in unserer Geschichte erreicht, wo ich mir sage, dass Gewalt nicht witzig oder anziehend wirken sollte."
Clint Eastwood

« Je ne fais pas amende honorable pour tous les personnages de films d'action que j'ai incarnés jusqu'à présent. Mais j'ai atteint un stade de ma vie et nous avons atteint un stade de notre histoire où je me dis que la violence ne doit plus être un objet de plaisanterie ni de convoitise. »
Clint Eastwood

STILL FROM 'IN THE LINE OF FIRE' (1993)
Female agent Rene Russo falls for ageing "dinosaur" Eastwood. / Agentin Raines (Rene Russo) verliebt sich in den alternden „Dinosaurier" Horrigan (Eastwood). / Sa jeune collègue (Rene Russo) succombe au charme du « dinosaure » Eastwood.

STILL FROM 'A PERFECT WORLD' (1993)
Criminologist Laura Dern and Texas Ranger Eastwood form an odd couple. / Die Kriminologin (Laura Dern) und der Texas-Ranger (Eastwood) bilden ein seltsames Paar. / Drôle de couple : la criminologue (Laura Dern) et le Texas Ranger (Eastwood).

STILL FROM 'A PERFECT WORLD' (1993)
Can escaped convict Kevin Costner be a father to kidnapped T.J. Lowther? / Kann der entflohene Strafgefangene (Kevin Costner) dem entführten „Buzz“ (T. J. Lowther) ein guter Vater sein? / Le prisonnier en cavale (Kevin Costner) peut-il être un père pour son otage (T. J. Lowther) ?

STILL FROM 'THE BRIDGES OF MADISON COUNTY' (1995)
Globe-trotting photographer Eastwood falls in love with Kansas housewife Meryl Streep. / Der vielgereiste Fotograf (Eastwood) verliebt sich in eine Hausfrau aus Kansas (Meryl Streep). / Le photographe globe-trotter (Eastwood) s'éprend de la femme au foyer (Meryl Streep).

STILL FROM 'THE BRIDGES OF MADISON COUNTY' (1995)
Meryl Streep's hand on Eastwood's shoulder speaks volumes about their love. / Meryl Streeps Hand auf Eastwoods Schulter spricht Bände über die Beziehung zwischen den beiden. / La main de Meryl Streep sur l'épaule d'Eastwood en dit plus qu'un long discours.

"I don't want to need you…'cause I can't have you."
Robert Kincaid (Clint Eastwood)

„Ich möchte dich nicht brauchen müssen …, weil ich dich nicht haben kann."
Robert Kincaid (Clint Eastwood)

« Je ne veux pas avoir besoin de toi… car je ne peux pas t'avoir. »
Robert Kincaid (Clint Eastwood)

STILL FROM 'ABSOLUTE POWER' (1997)
U.S. President Gene Hackman is responsible for Melora Hardin's death. / US-Präsident Richmond (Gene Hackman) hat Christy Sullivan (Melora Hardin) auf dem Gewissen. / Le Président des États-Unis (Gene Hackman) est responsable de la mort de Christy (Melora Hardin).

STILL FROM 'ABSOLUTE POWER' (1997)
Eastwood is a cat burglar who witnesses the President's crime. / Eastwood spielt einen Fassadenkletterer, der Augenzeuge des vom Präsidenten begangenen Verbrechens wird. / Eastwood en cambrioleur témoin du crime.

STILL FROM 'MIDNIGHT IN THE GARDEN OF GOOD AND EVIL' (1997)
Did fabulously wealthy Kevin Spacey (right) kill his gay lover Jude Law? / Hat der stinkreiche Williams (Kevin Spacey, rechts) seinen schwulen Liebhaber (Jude Law) getötet? / Le milliardaire (Kevin Spacey, à droite) a-t-il assassiné son jeune amant (Jude Law) ?

"The story is everything. If you don't have the material, the characters and the things to overcome and conflicts that give life to drama, you don't have it."
Clint Eastwood

„Die Geschichte ist das A und O. Wenn man keinen Stoff hat, keine Charaktere, keine Hindernisse, die es zu bewältigen gibt, und keine Konflikte, die ein Drama lebendig machen, dann hat man nichts."
Clint Eastwood

STILL FROM 'MIDNIGHT IN THE GARDEN OF GOOD AND EVIL' (1997)
Kevin Spacey shows John Cusack some voodoo in the graveyard. / Auf dem Friedhof zeigt Williams (Kevin Spacey) Kelso (John Cusack) ein paar Voodoo-Tricks. / Dans le cimetière, Kevin Spacey montre des rites vaudous à John Cusack.

« Tout repose sur l'intrigue. Si vous n'avez pas la matière, les personnages, les obstacles à surmonter et les conflits qui donnent vie à l'histoire, vous n'avez rien du tout. »
Clint Eastwood

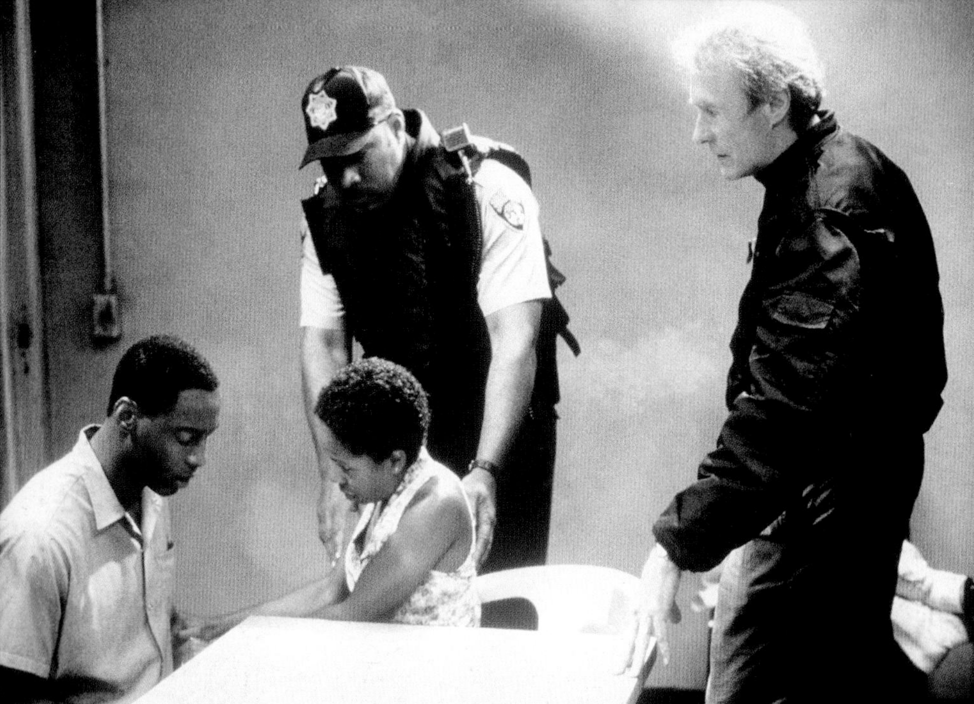

STILL FROM 'TRUE CRIME' (1999)
Death-row inmate Isaiah Washington has Eastwood as his last chance. / Für Todeskandidat Beechum (Isaiah Washington) ist Everett (Eastwood) die letzte Chance. / Le journaliste (Eastwood) offre sa dernière chance au condamné à mort (Isaiah Washington).

"It's not the kind of movie they're doing today, you know – it's hampered by having a story. But I think there's somebody out there who appreciates that, so I'll keep on trying."
Clint Eastwood

„Es ist nicht die Art von Film, die heutzutage gefragt ist, wissen Sie – er besitzt nämlich dummerweise eine Handlung. Aber ich glaube, es gibt noch Leute da draußen, die das zu schätzen wissen, und deshalb versuche ich es immer wieder."

STILL FROM 'TRUE CRIME' (1999)
Maverick reporter Eastwood gets a tongue-lashing from editor James Woods. / Der aufsässige Reporter (Eastwood) muss sich eine Standpauke von seinem Vorgesetzten (James Woods) anhören. / Eastwood se fait rappeler à l'ordre par son rédacteur en chef (James Woods).

STILL FROM 'SPACE COWBOYS' (2000)
Retired pilot Eastwood fulfills his dream of seeing Earth from space. / Der Pilot im Ruhestand Corvin (Eastwood) erfüllt sich seinen Wunsch, die Erde einmal aus dem Weltraum zu sehen. / Le pilote à la retraite (Eastwood) accomplit son rêve de voir la Terre de l'espace.

STILL FROM 'SPACE COWBOYS' (2000)
Unexpected astronauts James Garner, Tommy Lee Jones, Eastwood, Donald Sutherland. / James Garner, Tommy Lee Jones, Eastwood und Donald Sutherland werden überraschend Astronauten. / Un équipage insolite (James Garner, Tommy Lee Jones, Eastwood et Donald Sutherland).

„Die Gesellschaft hat uns eingeredet, wir sollten unser Leben lang wie ein 18-jähriges Model aussehen. Aber ich denke, ich kann genauso gut auch das sein, was ich bin."
Clint Eastwood

"Society has made us believe you should look like an 18-year-old model all your life. But I figure I might as well just be what I am."

« La société nous a fait croire que nous devions ressembler toute notre vie à un top-modèle de 18 ans. Mais moi, je pense que je peux tout aussi bien rester ce je suis. »

STILL FROM 'BLOOD WORK' (2002)
Eastwood: "I especially like McCaleb's vulnerability, both physically and psychologically." / „Mir gefällt an McCaleb besonders seine Verwundbarkeit, sowohl physisch als auch psychisch." (Eastwood) / « J'apprécie particulièrement la vulnérabilité de McCaleb, tant sur le plan physique que psychologique. » (Eastwood)

"It looks effortless, but it's very complicated to be simple. It's like [Clint Eastwood's] persona, which is very cool and calm, but there's a lot going on underneath it – there's a lot of passion, and a great deal of understanding of what it is to be human."
Martin Scorsese on Clint Eastwood

„Es sieht mühelos aus, aber es ist sehr kompliziert, einfach zu sein. Es ist wie [Clint Eastwoods] Persona, die sehr cool und ruhig ist, aber unter der Oberfläche tut sich viel – dort ist sehr viel Leidenschaft verborgen und eine ganze Menge Verständnis für das menschliche Wesen."
Martin Scorsese über Clint Eastwood

« Cela paraît facile, mais c'est très compliqué d'être simple. C'est comme le personnage [de Clint Eastwood], il est très froid et très calme, mais ça bouillonne en dessous, ça déborde de passion et de compréhension de ce que c'est qu'être humain. »
Martin Scorsese à propos de Clint Eastwood

STILL FROM 'BLOOD WORK' (2002)
Eastwood as a heart-transplant survivor tracking his donor's killer. / McCaleb (Eastwood) hat eine Herzverpflanzung überlebt und sucht nun den Mörder seines Spenders. / Eastwood en transplanté du cœur traquant l'assassin de son donneur.

"Has there ever been so unneurotic, so steadfast, and so steadily improving a moviemaker?"
David Thomson on Clint Eastwood

„Hat es jemals einen so unneurotischen, einen so standfesten und einen so stetig sich steigernden Filmemacher gegeben?"
David Thomson über Clint Eastwood

« A-t-on jamais vu un cinéaste aussi peu névrosé, aussi inébranlable et qui s'améliore de manière aussi constante ? »
David Thomson à propos de Clint Eastwood

PAGES 166/167
STILL FROM 'MYSTIC RIVER' (2003)
An Eastwood-directed film that questions Sean Penn's vigilante violence. / Ein Film unter Eastwoods Regie, der Jimmy Markums (Sean Penn) brutale Selbstjustiz infrage stellt. / Un film d'Eastwood qui remet en question la justice expéditive pratiquée par Sean Penn.

GYM RULES
Winners
are simply
willing to do
what losers
won't.
BOXEN

STILL FROM 'MILLION DOLLAR BABY' (2004)
Fight trainer Eastwood becomes coach and father figure to Hilary Swank. / Boxtrainer Frankie (Eastwood) wird Maggies (Hilary Swank) Coach und gleichzeitig ihr Ersatzvater. / L'entraîneur (Eastwood) devient une figure paternelle pour la jeune femme.

STILL FROM 'MILLION DOLLAR BABY' (2004)
Hilary Swank is determined to make it in a man's sport. / Maggie (Hilary Swank) ist entschlossen, sich in einem Männersport durchzusetzen. / Une boxeuse (Hilary Swank) déterminée à percer dans un univers masculin.

PAGES 170/171
STILL FROM 'MILLION DOLLAR BABY' (2004)
Eastwood and former boxer Morgan Freeman cheer on Hilary Swank. / Frankie (Eastwood) und Ex-Boxer Eddie (Morgan Freeman) feuern Maggie (Hilary Swank) an. / Eastwood et un ancien boxeur (Morgan Freeman) encouragent Hilary Swank.

STILL FROM 'MILLION DOLLAR BABY' (2004)
The climactic bout pitting Hilary Swank against Lucia Rijker. / Den Höhepunkt des Films bildet der Zweikampf zwischen Hilary Swank und Lucia Rijker. / Le combat décisif opposant Hilary Swank à Lucia Rijker.

PAGES 174/175
STILL FROM 'MILLION DOLLAR BABY' (2004)
An agonizing noir moment between Eastwood and Morgan Freeman. / Ein schmerzvoller, schwarzer Augenblick für Eastwood und Morgan Freeman. / Scène angoissante entre Eastwood et Morgan Freeman.

PAGES 176/177
STILL FROM 'FLAGS OF OUR FATHERS' (2006)
Raising the flag on Iwo Jima in World War II. / Das Aufstellen des Sternenbanners auf Iwo Jima im Zweiten Weltkrieg. / Lever de drapeau sur Iwo Jima pendant la Deuxième Guerre mondiale.

3

CHRONOLOGY

CHRONOLOGIE

CHRONOLOGIE

STILL FROM 'PLAY MISTY FOR ME' (1971)
Eastwood as a disc jockey at radio station KRML in Carmel, California. / Eastwood als Discjockey beim Rundfunksender KRML in Carmel in Kalifornien. / Eastwood en disc-jockey dans une station de radio californienne.

1930 Clinton Eastwood, Jr. is born on 31 May in San Francisco.

1946 Hears Charlie Parker at a concert in Oakland. Parker will later become the subject of an Eastwood film (*Bird*, 1988).

1953 Marries Maggie Johnson, a Berkeley graduate he first met on a blind date.

1955 Eastwood's film debut is a bit part in a sci-fi B-movie, *Revenge of the Creature*. This is followed by a small role in one of the Francis the Talking Mule films, *Francis in the Navy*.

1959–1966 The TV Western series *Rawhide* gives Eastwood one of his first major roles and puts him on the entertainment map.

1964 Achieves European stardom for his role as The Man with No Name in *A Fistful of Dollars*, the first of three spaghetti Westerns for director Sergio Leone.

1967 Forms his own production company, Malpaso, which will soon allow him greater creative control over his film projects and star image.

1968 *Coogan's Bluff* marks the first of five films that Eastwood will make with director Don Siegel.

1969 Makes his singing debut in the musical Western *Paint Your Wagon*, a film that goes so egregiously over budget it makes Eastwood vow to keep his own movies lean and economical.

1971 Takes a risk by playing a passive, victimized character in *The Beguiled*, which becomes his first box-office flop. *Play Misty for Me* - a one-night-stand revenge story like the later *Fatal Attraction* - is Eastwood's first feature-length film as a director.

PAGE 178
ON THE SET OF 'BREEZY' (1973)
Eastwood takes a sun break from directing duties. / Eastwood legt eine kurze Sonnenpause während der Regiearbeit ein. / Repos bien mérité pour le réalisateur.

Eastwood stars as a rogue cop in *Dirty Harry*, his first American smash hit and a film that will spawn four sequels.

1976 Due to creative differences, Eastwood removes director Philip Kaufman from *The Outlaw Josey Wales* and takes the helm himself, prompting the Director's Guild to instate the 'Eastwood rule' to prevent this kind of takeover in the future. Eastwood and co-star Sondra Locke begin what will become a long-term working and personal relationship.

1978 Against the advice of producers and friends, Eastwood co-stars with an orangutan in the comedy *Every Which Way But Loose*, which becomes a huge hit.

1979 Separates from his wife Maggie, and they divorce in 1984.

1980 Pokes fun at his image as a Western hero in the Capraesque comedy *Bronco Billy*. A major retrospective of Eastwood's films is mounted at New York's Museum of Modern Art, followed by another retrospective in 1985 at the Cinémathèque française in Paris.

1983 President Ronald Reagan threatens tax increasers with a veto by challenging them to "Go ahead, make my day," repeating Dirty Harry's line from *Sudden Impact*.

1984 Wins praise for *Tightrope* in which Eastwood walks a fine line between the cop he plays and the sex killer who is his double and alter ego. His real-life daughter Alison plays his daughter in the film.

1986–1988 Serves as mayor of Carmel, California in an effort to fight red tape and bureaucracy.

1989 Eastwood's chemistry with co-star Frances Fisher on *Pink Cadillac* leads to an off-screen romance.

1990 Eastwood, who is becoming a venerable director himself, plays John Huston in *White Hunter, Black Heart*, a movie about the making of *The African Queen*.

1992 The demythologizing Western *Unforgiven* is released to international acclaim, earning Eastwood real respect for the first time.

1993 *Unforgiven* is given the Academy Award for Best Picture, and Eastwood wins as Best Director. His 84-year-old mother Ruth is in attendance with him at the Oscar ceremony.

1996 Receives the American Film Institute's prestigious Life Achievement Award. Eastwood marries TV reporter Dina Ruiz. At a Carnegie Hall show called 'Eastwood After Hours, A Night of Jazz,' musicians honor him for the respect he has paid to jazz in his films.

2003 Wins the Life Achievement Award from the Screen Actors Guild.

2004 The Motion Picture Academy nominates *Mystic River* for Best Picture, and Eastwood for Best Director. *Million Dollar Baby* stirs up controversy with its euthanasia scene.

2005 Wins his second Best Director Oscar for *Million Dollar Baby*, which also wins Best Picture. Again, Eastwood's mother – now 96 years old – attends the ceremony.

2006 Agrees to develop a Dirty Harry video game with Warner Bros. Interactive Entertainment. Directs *Flags of Our Fathers* and prepares to direct *Red Sun, Black Sand* – two films that represent the different American and Japanese points of view on the Battle of Iwo Jima during World War Two.

CHRONOLOGIE

1930 Clinton Eastwood jr. wird am 31. Mai in San Francisco geboren.

1946 Er hört Charlie Parker auf einem Konzert in Oakland. Parker wird später das Thema eines Eastwood-Films (*Bird*, 1988).

1953 Heirat mit Maggie Johnson, die in Berkeley studiert und die er bei einem Blind Date kennen gelernt hatte.

1955 Eastwoods Filmdebüt ist eine Minirolle in dem zweitklassigen Science-Fiction-Streifen *Revenge of the Creature* (*Rache des Ungeheuers*). Dem folgt eine kleine Rolle in *Francis in the Navy*, einem von mehreren Filmen mit „Francis, dem sprechenden Maultier".

1959–1966 In der Fernsehwesternserie *Rawhide* (*Cowboys/Tausend Meilen Staub*) erhält Eastwood eine seiner ersten großen Rollen und macht sich in der Unterhaltungsindustrie einen Namen.

1964 Durch seine Rolle als „Namenloser" in *Per un pugno di dollari* (*Für eine Handvoll Dollar*), dem ersten von drei Spaghettiwestern unter der Regie von Sergio Leone, wird er in Europa zum Star.

1967 Er gründet seine eigene Produktionsfirma Malpaso, die ihm bald eine größere kreative Kontrolle über seine Filmprojekte und sein Image als Star gibt.

1968 *Coogan's Bluff* (*Coogans großer Bluff*) ist der erste von fünf Filmen, die Eastwood mit Regisseur Don Siegel dreht.

1969 In dem Musical-Western *Paint Your Wagon* (*Westwärts zieht der Wind*) gibt er sein Debüt als Sänger. Aus der Tatsache, dass der Film sein Budget maßlos überzieht, zieht er die Konsequenz, seine eigenen Filme schlank und wirtschaftlich zu drehen.

1971 Geht das Risiko ein, eine passive Opferrolle in *The Beguiled* (*Betrogen*) zu spielen, seinem ersten Flop an der Kinokasse. Eastwoods erster Spielfilm als Regisseur, *Play Misty for Me* (*Sadistico – Wunschkonzert für einen Toten*), ist eine Rachegeschichte nach einem One-Night-Stand, ähnlich wie später *Fatal Attraction* (*Eine verhängnisvolle Affäre*). Er spielt einen einzelgängerischen Polizisten in *Dirty Harry*; sein erster Kassenschlager in den USA ist der Auftakt zu einer fünfteiligen Reihe um den gleichnamigen Protagonisten.

1976 Aufgrund kreativer Meinungsverschiedenheiten feuert Eastwood Philip Kaufman, den Regisseur des Films *The Outlaw Josey Wales* (*Der Texaner*), und übernimmt selbst die Regie. Daraufhin führt die Regisseurgewerkschaft (DGA) die „Eastwood-Regel" ein, die eine solche Übernahme künftig verhindern soll. Eastwood und seine Kollegin Sondra Locke beginnen eine langjährige private und berufliche Beziehung.

1978 Gegen den Rat von Produzenten und Freunden spielt Eastwood neben einem Orang-Utan die Hauptrolle in der Komödie *Every Which Way But Loose* (*Der Mann aus San Fernando*), die zu einem Riesenhit wird.

1979 Trennung von seiner Frau Maggie, von der er sich 1984 scheiden lässt.

1980 Macht sich über sein Image als Westernheld in der capraesken Komödie *Bronco Billy* lustig. Das New Yorker Museum of Moderne Art (MoMA) zeigt eine umfangreiche Retrospektive von Eastwood-Filmen. 1985 folgt eine weitere Retrospektive an der Cinémathèque française in Paris.

1983 Der amerikanische Präsident und Ex-Schauspieler Ronald Reagan droht Politikern, die die Steuern erhöhen wollen, mit einem Veto und zitiert dabei „Dirty" Harrys Worte „Go ahead, make my day" aus *Sudden Impact* (*Dirty Harry kommt zurück*).

1984 Er wird von Kritikern für *Tightrope* (*Der Wolf hetzt die Meute*) gelobt, wo er auf einem schmalen Grat wandelt bei der Darstellung von einem Cop und seinem Doppelgänger und Alter Ego, einem Triebmörder. Eastwoods Tochter Alison spielt auch im Film seine Tochter.

1986–1988 Bürgermeister des kalifornischen Küstenstädtchens Carmel, wo er übermäßige Bürokratie bekämpft.

1989 Die „Chemie" zu Frances Fisher, seiner Kollegin und Mitdarstellerin aus *Pink Cadillac*, führt zu einer Beziehung.

1990 Eastwood, der sich selbst zu einem angesehenen Regisseur mausert, spielt John Huston (als Wilson) in *White Hunter, Black Heart* (*Weißer*

STILL FROM 'HONKYTONK MAN' (1982)
Dying while recording the songs that will make his name. / Er stirbt bei der Aufnahme der Lieder, die ihn berühmt machen werden. / Foudroyé pendant l'enregistrement des chansons qui le rendront célèbre.

Jäger, schwarzes Herz). Der Film handelt von der Entstehung des Klassikers *The African Queen* (*African Queen*).

1992 Der Anti-Western *Unforgiven* (*Erbarmungslos*) stößt weltweit auf positive Resonanz und bringt Eastwood erstmals echte Anerkennung.

1993 *Unforgiven* (*Erbarmungslos*) erhält den Oscar als bester Film, während Eastwood für die beste Regie ausgezeichnet wird. Seine 84-jährige Mutter Ruth ist bei der Verleihung anwesend.

1996 Erhält den renommierten „Life Achievement Award" des Amerikanischen Filminstituts (AFI) für sein Lebenswerk. Eastwood heiratet die Fernsehreporterin Dina Ruiz. In der Show „Eastwood After Hours: A Night of Jazz" in der New Yorker Carnegie Hall ehren ihn Musiker für die Würdigung der Jazzmusik in seinen Filmen.

2003 Erhält den renommierten „Life Achievement Award" der Schauspielergewerkschaft (SAG) für sein Lebenswerk.

2004 Die Filmakademie (AMPAS) nominiert *Mystic River* als besten Film und Eastwood für die beste Regie. *Million Dollar Baby* löst mit seiner Euthanasieszene Kontroversen aus.

2005 Erhält zum zweiten Mal einen Oscar für die beste Regie in *Million Dollar Baby*, der auch als bester Film des Jahres ausgezeichnet wird. Auch diesmal sitzt Eastwoods mittlerweile 96-jährige Mutter bei der Verleihung im Publikum.

2006 Stimmt der Entwicklung eines *Dirty-Harry*-Videospiels für Warner Bros. Interactive Entertainment zu. Führt Regie bei *Flags of Our Fathers* und bereitet *Red Sun, Black Sand* vor. Die beiden Filme zeigen die Schlacht von Iwo Jima im Zweiten Weltkrieg aus dem amerikanischen und dem japanischen Blickwinkel.

CHRONOLOGIE

1930 Clinton Eastwood junior naît le 31 mai à San Francisco.

1946 Assiste à un concert de Charlie Parker, auquel il consacrera par la suite un film (*Bird*, 1988).

1953 Épouse Maggie Johnson, une diplômée de Berkeley rencontrée lors d'un rendez-vous arrangé.

1955 Fait ses débuts au cinéma avec un rôle de figurant dans un film de science-fiction de série B, *La Revanche de la créature*. Obtient ensuite un petit rôle dans l'une des aventures de « Francis la mule qui parle », *Francis in the Navy*.

1959–1966 La série télévisée *Rawhide* lui donne l'un de ses premiers grands rôles et le fait connaître du public.

1964 Connaît la célébrité en Europe grâce au rôle de l'Homme sans nom dans *Pour une poignée de dollars*, le premier d'une série de trois westerns spaghetti réalisés par Sergio Leone.

1967 Crée sa propre société de production, Malpaso, qui lui permettra de mieux contrôler ses projets et son image.

1968 *Un Shérif à New York* est le premier des cinq films que Eastwood va tourner avec le réalisateur Don Siegel.

1969 Fait ses débuts de chanteur avec la comédie musicale *La Kermesse de l'Ouest*, film qui dépasse le budget de manière si astronomique que Eastwood se jure de se montrer économe dans ses propres réalisations.

1971 Prend un risque en incarnant un personnage passif et persécuté dans *Les Proies*, son premier échec au box-office. *Un frisson dans la nuit* – une histoire de revanche sur une liaison sans lendemain qui sera reprise dans *Fatal Attraction* – est son premier long métrage en tant que réalisateur. Eastwood incarne un justicier sans scrupules dans *L'Inspecteur Harry*, son premier grand succès américain, qui donnera lieu à quatre suites.

1976 En raison de désaccords artistiques, Eastwood retire à Philip Kaufman la réalisation de *Josey Wales hors-la-loi* pour en prendre les commandes, ce qui conduit la Director's Guild à instaurer la « règle Eastwood » interdisant ce genre de pratiques. Eastwood et sa partenaire Sondra Locke entament une longue relation professionnelle et personnelle.

1978 Contre l'avis des producteurs et de ses amis, Eastwood partage l'affiche avec un orang-outan dans la comédie *Doux, dur et dingue*, qui connaît un immense succès.

1979 Se sépare de sa femme Maggie, dont il divorcera en 1984.

1980 Tourne en dérision son image de héros de western dans la comédie « capraesque » *Bronco Billy*. Une vaste rétrospective de ses œuvres est organisée au Museum of Modern Art de New York, suivie d'une autre en 1985 à la Cinémathèque de Paris.

1983 Le président Ronald Reagan menace d'opposer son veto à la hausse des impôts en lançant à ses adversaires « Allez-y, faites-moi plaisir », célèbre réplique de Clint Eastwood dans *Le Retour de l'inspecteur Harry*.

1984 Est salué pour son interprétation dans *La Corde raide*, où il jongle avec finesse entre son rôle de policier et celui du maniaque sexuel qui est son alter ego. Sa fille Alison joue le rôle de sa fille dans le film.

1986–1988 Se fait élire maire de Carmel, en Californie, pour tenter de lutter contre la bureaucratie.

1989 L'alchimie qui opère avec Frances Fisher, sa partenaire dans *Pink Cadillac*, donne naissance à une liaison à la ville comme à l'écran.

1990 Eastwood, lui-même devenu un vénérable metteur en scène, incarne John Huston dans *Chasseur blanc, cœur noir*, un film retraçant le tournage d'*African Queen*.

1992 *Impitoyable* brise le mythe du western et est salué par la critique internationale, dont Eastwood gagne ainsi le respect.

1993 *Impitoyable* reçoit l'oscar du Meilleur film et Eastwood celui du Meilleur réalisateur. Sa mère Ruth, âgée de 84 ans, l'accompagne à la cérémonie de remise.

ON THE SET OF 'BIRD' (1988)
Eastwood directs Forest Whitaker as tormented jazz genius Charlie Parker. / Eastwood gibt Forest Whitaker, der das gequälte Jazzgenie Charlie Parker spielt, Anweisungen. / Sous la direction d'Eastwood, Forest Whitaker incarne un génie torturé, Charlie Parker.

1996 Reçoit le prestigieux prix de l'American Film Institute récompensant l'ensemble de sa carrière. Épouse la journaliste de télévision Dina Ruiz. Lors d'un concert au Carnegie Hall intitulé « Eastwood After Hours, A Night of Jazz », des musiciens lui rendent hommage pour la place que le jazz occupe dans ses films.

2003 Remporte le prix de la Screen Actors Guild pour l'ensemble de son œuvre.

2004 *Mystic River* est nommé pour l'oscar du Meilleur film et Eastwood pour celui du Meilleur réalisateur. *Million Dollar Baby* suscite la controverse avec une scène d'euthanasie.

2005 Remporte son deuxième oscar du Meilleur réalisateur pour *Million Dollar Baby*, également sacré Meilleur film. Sa mère, désormais âgée de 96 ans, assiste une nouvelle fois à la cérémonie.

2006 Accepte de créer un jeu vidéo inspiré de *L'Inspecteur Harry* avec Warner Bros. Interactive Entertainment. Réalise *Flags of Our Fathers* et prépare le tournage de *Red Sun, Black Sand*, deux films qui présentent respectivement le point de vue des Américains et celui des Japonais lors de la bataille d'Iwo Jima, durant la Seconde Guerre mondiale.

CLINT
EASTWOOD
IN UN FILM DI
SERGIO LEONE
PRODUZIONE · DISTRIBUZIONE
PEA
PER QUALCHE DOLLARO IN PIÙ
CON LEE VAN CLEEF · GIAN MARIA VOLONTE'
MARA KRUP LUIGI PISTILLI KLAUS KINSKI JOSEF EGGER PANOS PAPADOPULOS BENITO STEFANELLI ROBERT CAMARDIEL ALDO SAMBRELL LUIS RODRIGUEZ MARIO BREGA
TECHNICOLOR · TECHNISCOPE

4

FILMOGRAPHY

FILMOGRAFIE

FILMOGRAPHIE

***Revenge of the Creature/Rache des Ungeheuers/ La Revanche de la créature* (1955)** Eastwood appears uncredited as a lab technician./Eastwood tritt ohne Erwähnung als Labortechniker auf./Apparition - non créditée - en technicien de laboratoire.

***Francis in the Navy* (1955)** Eastwood appears as Jonesy./Eastwood tritt als Jonesy auf./Apparition dans le rôle de Jonesy.

***Lady Godiva of Coventry/Nackte Geisel/Lady Godiva of Coventry* (1955)** Eastwood appears uncredited as a Saxon./Eastwood tritt ohne Erwähnung als Sachse auf./Apparition - non créditée - dans le rôle d'un Saxon.

***Tarantula* (1955)** Eastwood appears uncredited as Jet Squadron Leader./Eastwood tritt ohne Erwähnung als Anführer eines Jagdgeschwaders auf./Apparition - non créditée - en chef d'escadron.

***Highway Patrol* (1956)** TV series/Fernsehserie/série TV. Eastwood appears as Motorcycle Gang Leader in 'Motorcycle A' episode./Eastwood tritt in der Folge „Motorcycle A" als als Anführer der Motorradbande auf./Apparition en chef de gang de motards dans l'épisode « Motorcycle A ».

***Never Say Goodbye/Nur du allein/Ne dites jamais adieu* (1956)** Eastwood appears uncredited as Will./ Eastwood tritt ohne Erwähnung als Will auf./ Apparition - non créditée - dans le rôle de Will.

***Star in the Dust (Law Man)/Noch heute sollst Du hängen/La corde est prête* (1956)** Eastwood appears uncredited as Tom, ranch hand./Eastwood tritt ohne Erwähnung als Rancharbeiter Tom auf./ Apparition - non créditée - dans le rôle de Tom, employé de ranch.

***Away All Boats/Klar Schiff zum Gefecht/Brisants humains* (1956)** Eastwood appears uncredited as a Marine medic./Eastwood tritt ohne Erwähnung als Schiffssanitäter auf./Apparition - non créditée - en médecin de la Marine.

***The First Traveling Saleslady/The First Traveling Saleslady/La VRP de choc* (1956)** Eastwood appears as Lt. Jack Rice, roughrider./Eastwood tritt als Zureiter Lieutenant Jack Rice auf./Apparition dans le rôle du lieutenant Jack Rice, dresseur de chevaux.

***Death Valley Days/Der wilde Westen/Death Valley Days* (1956)** TV series/Fernsehserie/série TV. Eastwood appears as John Lucas in 'The Last Letter' episode./Eastwood tritt in der Folge „The Last Letter" als John Lucas auf./Apparition dans le rôle de John Lucas dans l'épisode « The Last Letter ».

***West Point* (1957)** TV series/Fernsehserie/série TV. Eastwood appears in 'White Fury' episode./ Eastwood tritt in der Folge „White Fury" auf./ Apparition dans l'épisode « White Fury ».

***Escapade in Japan/Verschollen in Japan/Escapade au Japon* (1957)** Eastwood appears uncredited as Dumbo Pilot./Eastwood tritt ohne Erwähnung als Dumbo-Pilot auf./Apparition - non créditée - en pilote.

***Navy Log* (1958)** TV series/Fernsehserie/série TV. Eastwood appears as Burns in 'The Lonely Watch' episode./Eastwood tritt in der Folge „The Lonely Watch" als Burns auf./Apparition dans le rôle de Burns dans l'épisode « The Lonely Watch ».

***Lafayette Escadrille/Lafayette Escadrille/C'est la guerre* (1956)** Eastwood appears as George Moseley./ Eastwood tritt als George Moseley auf./Apparition dans le rôle de George Moseley.

***Ambush at Cimarron Pass* (1958)** Eastwood appears as Keith Williams./Eastwood tritt als Keith Williams auf./Apparition dans le rôle de Keith Williams.

***Maverick* (1959)** TV series/Fernsehserie/série TV. Eastwood appears as Red Hardigan in 'Duel at Sundown' episode./Eastwood tritt in der Folge „Duel at Sundown" als Red Hardigan auf./Apparition dans le rôle de Red Hardigan dans l'épisode « Duel au soleil couchant ».

***Rawhide/Cowboys (a. Tausend Meilen Staub)/ Rawhide* (1959–1966)** TV series/Fernsehserie/série TV. Eastwood stars as Rowdy Yates./Eastwood spielt als Rowdy Yates eine der Hauptrollen der Serie./Dans le rôle de Rowdy Yates

***A Fistful of Dollars (Per un pugno di dollari)/Für eine Handvoll Dollar/Pour une poignée de dollars* (1964)** Eastwood stars as Joe – aka The Man with No Name./Eastwood spielt als Joe – alias „Der Namenlose" – eine Hauptrolle./Dans le rôle de Joe – alias l'Homme sans nom.

***For a Few Dollars More (Per qualche dollaro in più)/Für ein paar Dollar mehr/Et pour quelques dollars de plus* (1964)** Eastwood stars as Monco – aka The Man with No Name./Eastwood spielt als Monco – alias „Der Namenlose" – eine Hauptrolle./ dans le rôle de Monco – alias l'Homme sans nom.

***The Witches (Le Streghe)/Hexen von heute/Les Sorcières* (1965)** Eastwood appears as Charlie./ Eastwood tritt als Charlie auf./Apparition dans le rôle de Charlie.

***The Good, the Bad and the Ugly (Il buono, il brutto, il cattivo)/Zwei glorreiche Halunken/Le Bon, la Brute et le Truand* (1966)** Eastwood stars as Joe – aka The Man with No Name./Eastwood spielt als Blondie – alias „Der Namenlose" – eine Hauptrolle./ dans le rôle de Blondie – alias l'Homme sans nom.

***Hang 'Em High/Hängt ihn höher/Pendez-les haut et court* (1968)** Eastwood stars as Marshal Jed Cooper./Eastwood spielt als Marshal Jed Cooper eine Hauptrolle./Dans le rôle du marshal Jed Cooper.

***Coogan's Bluff/Coogans großer Bluff/Un shérif à New York* (1968)** Eastwood stars as Deputy Sheriff Walt Coogan./Eastwood spielt als Hilfssheriff Walt Coogan die Titelrolle./Dans le rôle du shérif adjoint Walt Coogan.

***Where Eagles Dare/Agenten sterben einsam/ Quand les aigles attaquent* (1968)** Eastwood stars as Lt. Morris Schaffer./Eastwood spielt als Lieutenant Morris Schaffer eine Hauptrolle./Dans le rôle du lieutenant Morris Schaffer.

***Paint Your Wagon/Westwärts zieht der Wind/ La Kermesse de l'Ouest* (1969)** Eastwood stars as Pardner./Eastwood spielt als Pardner eine Hauptrolle./Dans le rôle de Pardner.

***Two Mules for Sister Sara/Ein Fressen für die Geier/Sierra torride* (1970)** Eastwood stars as Hogan./Eastwood spielt als Hogan eine Hauptrolle./ dans le rôle de Hogan.

***Kelly's Heroes/Stoßtrupp Gold/De l'or pour les braves* (1970)** Eastwood stars as Pvt. Kelly./Eastwood spielt als Gefreiter Kelly eine Hauptrolle./Dans le rôle du soldat Kelly.

***The Beguiled/Betrogen/Les Proies* (1971)** Eastwood stars as Cpl. John McBurney./Eastwood spielt als Corporal John McBurney eine Hauptrolle./Dans le rôle du caporal John McBurney.

***Play Misty for Me/Sadistico – Wunschkonzert für einen Toten/Un frisson dans la nuit* (1971)** Eastwood directs and stars as David 'Dave' Garver./Eastwood führt Regie und spielt als David „Dave" Garver eine Hauptrolle./Réalisation et rôle de Dave Garver.

***Dirty Harry/Dirty Harry/L'Inspecteur Harry* (1971)** Eastwood stars as Insp. Harry Callahan./Eastwood spielt als Inspektor „Dirty" Harry Callahan die Titelrolle./Dans le rôle de l'inspecteur Harry Callahan.

***Joe Kidd/Sinola/Joe Kidd* (1972)** Eastwood stars as Joe Kidd./Eastwood spielt als Joe Kidd die Hauptrolle./Dans le rôle de Joe Kidd.

***High Plains Drifter/Ein Fremder ohne Namen/ L'Homme des hautes plaines* (1973)** Eastwood directs and stars as The Stranger./Eastwood führt Regie und spielt als „Fremder" die Hauptrolle./ Réalisation et rôle de l'Étranger.

***Magnum Force/Calahan/Magnum Force* (1973)** Eastwood stars as Insp. 'Dirty' Harry Callahan./ Eastwood spielt als Inspektor „Dirty" Harry Callahan eine Hauptrolle./Dans le rôle de l'inspecteur Harry Callahan.

***Breezy/Begegnung am Vormittag/Breezy* (1973)** Eastwood directs./Eastwood führt Regie./Réalisation.

***Thunderbolt and Lightfoot/Die letzten beißen die Hunde/Le Canardeur* (1974)** Eastwood stars as John 'Thunderbolt' Doherty./Eastwood spielt als John „Thunderbolt" Doherty eine der beiden Titelrollen./Dans le rôle de John Doherty alias Thunderbolt.

***The Eiger Sanction/Im Auftrag des Drachen/La Sanction* (1975)** Eastwood directs and stars as Dr. Jonathan Hemlock./Eastwood führt Regie und spielt als Dr. Jonathan Hemlock eine Hauptrolle./réalisation et rôle du Dr Jonathan Hemlock.

***The Outlaw Josey Wales/Der Texaner/Josey Wales hors-la-loi* (1976)** Eastwood directs and stars as Josey Wales./Eastwood führt Regie und spielt als Josey Wales die Hauptrolle./réalisation et rôle de Josey Wales.

***The Enforcer/Der Unerbittliche/L'inspecteur ne renonce jamais* (1976)** Eastwood stars as Insp. 'Dirty' Harry Callahan./Eastwood spielt als Inspektor „Dirty" Harry Callahan die Hauptrolle./Dans le rôle de l'inspecteur Harry Callahan.

***The Gauntlet/Der Mann, der niemals aufgibt/L'Épreuve de force* (1977)** Eastwood directs and stars as Ben Shockley./Eastwood führt Regie und spielt als Ben Shockley eine Hauptrolle./réalisation et rôle de Ben Shockley.

***Every Which Way But Loose/Der Mann aus San Fernando/Doux, dur et dingue* (1978)** Eastwood stars as Philo Beddoe./Eastwood spielt als Philo Beddoe eine Hauptrolle./Dans le rôle de Philo Beddoe.

***Escape from Alcatraz/Flucht von Alcatraz/L'Évadé d'Alcatraz* (1979)** Eastwood stars as Frank Morris./Eastwood spielt als Frank Morris eine Hauptrolle./dans le rôle de Frank Morris.

***Bronco Billy* (1980)** Eastwood directs and stars as Bronco Billy McCoy./Eastwood führt Regie und spielt als „Bronco" Billy McCoy die Titelrolle./réalisation et rôle de Bronco Billy McCoy.

***Any Which Way You Can/Mit Vollgas nach San Fernando/Ça va cogner* (1980)** Eastwood stars as Philo Beddoe./Eastwood spielt als Philo Beddoe eine Hauptrolle./Dans le rôle de Philo Beddoe.

***Firefox/Firefox/Firefox, l'arme absolue* (1982)** Eastwood directs and stars as Mitchell Gant./Eastwood führt Regie und spielt als Mitchell Gant eine Hauptrolle./Réalisation et rôle de Mitchell Gant.

***Honkytonk Man* (1982)** Eastwood directs and stars as Red Stovall./Eastwood führt Regie und spielt als Red Stovall eine Hauptrolle./Réalisation et rôle de Red Stovall.

***Sudden Impact/Dirty Harry kommt zurück/Le Retour de l'inspecteur Harry* (1983)** Eastwood directs and stars as Insp. 'Dirty' Harry Callahan./Eastwood führt Regie und spielt als Inspektor „Dirty" Harry Callahan eine Hauptrolle./Réalisation et rôle de l'inspecteur Harry Callahan.

***Tightrope/Der Wolf hetzt die Meute/La Corde raide* (1984)** Eastwood directs - uncredited - and stars as Wes Block./Eastwood führt Regie - ohne Erwähnung - und spielt als Captain Wes Block eine Hauptrolle./Réalisation - non créditée - et rôle de l'inspecteur Wes Block.

***City Heat/City Heat - Der Bulle und der Schnüffler/Haut les flingues* (1984)** Eastwood stars as Lieutenant Speer./Eastwood spielt als Lieutenant Speer eine Hauptrolle./Dans le rôle du lieutenant Speer.

***Pale Rider/Pale Rider - Der namenlose Reiter/Pale Rider, le cavalier solitaire* (1985)** Eastwood directs and stars as Preacher./Eastwood führt Regie und spielt als Prediger eine Hauptrolle./Réalisation et rôle du pasteur.

***Amazing Stories/Unglaubliche Geschichten/Histoires fantastiques* (1985)** TV series/Fernsehserie/série TV.Eastwood directs 'Vanessa in the Garden' episode./Eastwood führt Regie bei der Folge „Vanessa in the Garden" - „Verliebt in die Kunst"/Réalisation de l'épisode « Vanessa in the Garden ».

***Heartbreak Ridge/Heartbreak Ridge/Le Maître de guerre* (1986)** Eastwood directs and stars as Gunnery Sgt. Tom 'Gunny' Highway./Eastwood führt Regie und spielt als Gunnery Sergeant Tom „Gunny" Highway eine Hauptrolle./Réalisation et rôle du sergent Tom - alias « Gunny » Highway.

***The Dead Pool/Das Todesspiel/La Dernière Cible* (1988)** Eastwood stars as Insp. 'Dirty' Harry Callahan./Eastwood spielt als Inspektor „Dirty" Harry Callahan eine Hauptrolle./Dans le rôle de l'inspecteur Harry Callahan.

***Bird* (1988)** Eastwood directs./Eastwood führt Regie./Réalisation.

***Pink Cadillac* (1989)** Eastwood stars as Tommy Nowak./Eastwood spielt als Tommy Nowak eine Hauptrolle./Dans le rôle de Tommy Nowak.

***White Hunter, Black Heart/Weißer Jäger, schwarzes Herz/Chasseur blanc, cœur noir* (1990)** Eastwood directs and stars as John Wilson./Eastwood führt Regie und spielt als John Wilson eine Hauptrolle./Réalisation et rôle de John Wilson.

***The Rookie/Rookie - Der Anfänger/La Relève* (1990)** Eastwood directs and stars as Nick Pulovski./Eastwood führt Regie und spielt als Nick Pulovski eine Hauptrolle./Réalisation et rôle de Nick Pulovski.

***Unforgiven/Erbarmungslos/Impitoyable* (1992)** Eastwood directs and stars as William 'Bill' Munny./Eastwood führt Regie und spielt als William „Bill" Munny eine Hauptrolle./Réalisation et rôle de William alias « Bill » Munny.

***In the Line of Fire/In the Line of Fire - Die zweite Chance/Dans la ligne de mire* (1993)** Eastwood stars as Secret Service Agent Frank Horrigan./Eastwood spielt als Geheimagent Frank Horrigan eine Hauptrolle./Dans le rôle de l'agent secret Frank Horrigan.

***A Perfect World/Perfect World/Un monde parfait* (1993)** Eastwood directs and stars as Chief Red Garnett./Eastwood führt Regie und spielt als Chief Red Garnett eine Hauptrolle./Réalisation et rôle de Red Garnett.

***The Bridges of Madison County/Die Brücken am Fluß/Sur la route de Madison* (1995)** Eastwood directs and stars as Robert Kincaid./Eastwood führt Regie und spielt als Robert Kincaid eine Hauptrolle./Réalisation et rôle de Robert Kincaid.

***Absolute Power/Absolute Power/Les Pleins Pouvoirs* (1997)** Eastwood directs and stars as Luther Whitney./Eastwood führt Regie und spielt als Luther Whitney eine Hauptrolle./Réalisation et rôle de Luther Whitney.

***Midnight in the Garden of Good and Evil/Mitternacht im Garten von Gut und Böse/Minuit dans le jardin du bien et du mal* (1997)** Eastwood directs./Eastwood führt Regie./Réalisation.

***True Crime/Ein wahres Verbrechen/Jugé coupable* (1999)** Eastwood directs and stars as Steve Everett./Eastwood führt Regie und spielt als Steve Everett eine Hauptrolle./Réalisation et rôle de Steve Everett.

***Space Cowboys*(2000)** Eastwood directs and stars as Frank Corvin./Eastwood führt Regie und spielt als Frank Corvin eine Hauptrolle./Réalisation et rôle de Frank Corvin.

***Blood Work/Blood Work/Créance de sang* (2002)** Eastwood directs and stars as Terry McCaleb./Eastwood führt Regie und spielt als Terry McCaleb eine Hauptrolle./Réalisation et rôle de Terry McCaleb.

***Mystic River* (2003)** Eastwood directs./Eastwood führt Regie./Réalisation.

The Blues/The Blues/Du Mali au Mississippi (TV series/Fernsehserie/série TV, **2003**) Eastwood directs 'Piano Blues' episode./Eastwood führt Regie bei der Folge „Piano Blues"./Réalisation de l'épisode « Piano Blues ».

***Million Dollar Baby* (2004)** Eastwood directs and stars as Frankie Dunn./Eastwood führt Regie und spielt als Frankie Dunn eine Hauptrolle./Réalisation et rôle de Frankie Dunn.

***Flags of Our Fathers* (2006)** Eastwood directs./Eastwood führt Regie./Réalisation.

BIBLIOGRAPHY

Beard, William: *Persistence of Double Vision: Essays on Clint Eastwood*. University of Alberta Press, 2000.
Bingham, Dennis: *Acting Male: Masculinities in the Films of James Stewart, Jack Nicholson, and Clint Eastwood*. Rutgers University Press, 1994.
Brion, Patrick: *Clint Eastwood: Biographie, filmographie illustrée, analyse critique*. De la Martinière, 2002.
Buscombe, Edward: *Unforgiven*. BFI, 2004.
Carlson, Michael: *Clint Eastwood*. Pocket Essentials, 2002.
Casas, Quinn: *Clint Eastwood: Avatares del último cineasta clásico*. Jaguar, 2003.
Clinch, Minty: *Clint Eastwood: A Biography*. Hodder & Stoughton, 1994.
Frayling, Christopher: *Clint Eastwood*. Virgin, 1992.
Frayling, Christopher: *Once upon a Time in Italy: The Westerns of Sergio Leone*. Harry N. Abrams, 2005.
Frayling, Christopher: *Sergio Leone: Something to Do with Death*. Faber & Faber, 2000.
Gallafent, Edward: *Clint Eastwood: Filmmaker and Star*. Continuum, 1994.
Guérif, François: *Clint Eastwood*. St. Martin's Press, 1986.
Johnstone, Iain: *The Man with No Name: Clint Eastwood*. Quill/William Morrow, 1988.
Kapsis, Robert E. & Coblentz, Kathie (Eds.): *Clint Eastwood: Interviews*. University Press of Mississippi, 1999.
Kitses, Jim: *Horizons West: Directing the Western from John Ford to Clint Eastwood*. University of California Press 2004.
Knapp, Laurence F.: *Directed by Clint Eastwood: Eighteen Films Analyzed*. McFarland, 1996.
Locke, Sondra: *The Good, the Bad & the Very Ugly: A Hollywood Journey*. William Morrow, 1997.
McGilligan, Patrick: *Clint: The Life and Legend*. St. Martin's Press, 2002.
Midding, Gerhard: *Clint Eastwood: Der konservative Rebell*. Uwe Wiedleroither, 1996.
Munn, Michael: *Clint Eastwood: Hollywood's Loner*. Robson, 1993.
O'Brien, Daniel: *Clint Eastwood: Film-Maker*. B.T. Batsford, 1996.
Pfeiffer, Lee & Lewis, Michael: *The Ultimate Clint Eastwood Trivia Book*. Citadel, 1996.
Schickel, Richard: *Clint Eastwood: A Biography*. Knopf, 1996.
Simsolo, Noël: *Clint Eastwood: Un passeur à Hollywood*. Cahiers du cinéma, 2003.
Smith, Paul: *Clint Eastwood: A Cultural Production*. University of Minnesota Press, 1993.
Tanitch, Robert: *Clint Eastwood*. Studio Vista, 1995.
Thompson, Douglas: *Clint Eastwood: Billion Dollar Man*. John Blake, 2005.
Thompson, Douglas: *Clint Eastwood: Riding High*. Contemporary Books, 1992.
Zmijewsky, Boris & Pfeiffer, Lee: *The Films of Clint Eastwood, 1955-1993*. Citadel Press, 1993.

IMPRINT

Hohenzollernring 53, D-50672 Köln
www.taschen.com

Editor/Picture Research/Layout: Paul Duncan/Wordsmith Solutions
Editorial Coordination: Martin Holz, Cologne
Production Coordination: Nadia Najm and Horst Neuzner, Cologne
German translation: Thomas J. Kinne, Nauheim
French translation: Anne Le Bot, Paris
Multilingual production: www.arnaudbriand.com, Paris
Typeface Design: Sense/Net, Andy Disl and Birgit Reber, Cologne

Printed in Italy
ISBN-13: 978-3-8228-2004-9
ISBN-10: 3-8228-2004-0

All the photos in this book were supplied by The Kobal Collection.